Elizabeth Bowen

THE IRISH WRITERS SERIES
James F. Carens, General Editor

EIMAR O'DUFFY	Robert Hogan
J. C. MANGAN	James Kilroy
J. M. SYNGE	Robin Skelton
PAUL VINCENT CARROLL	Paul A. Doyle
SEAN O'CASEY	Bernard Benstock
SEUMAS O'KELLY	George Brandon Saul
SHERIDAN LEFANU	Michael Begnal
SOMERVILLE AND ROSS	John Cronin
STANDISH O'GRADY	Phillip L. Marcus
SUSAN L. MITCHELL	Richard M. Kain
W. R. RODGERS	Darcy O'Brien
MERVYN WALL	Robert Hogan
LADY GREGORY	Hazard Adams
LIAM O'FLAHERTY	James O'Brien
MARIA EDGEWORTH	James Newcomer
SIR SAMUEL FERGUSON	Malcolm Brown
BRIAN FRIEL	D. E. S. Maxwell
PEADAR O'DONNELL	Grattan Freyer
DANIEL CORKERY	George Brandon Saul
BENEDICT KIELY	Daniel Casey
CHARLES ROBERT MATURIN	Robert E. Lougy
DOUGLAS HYDE	Gareth Dunleavy
EDNA O'BRIEN	Grace Eckley
FRANCIS STUART	J. H. Natterstad
JOHN BUTLER YEATS	Douglas N. Archibald
JOHN MONTAGUE	Frank Kersnowski
KATHARINE TYNAN	Marilyn Gaddis Rose
BRIAN MOORE	Jeanne Flood
PATRICK KAVANAGH	Darcy O'Brien
OLIVER ST. JOHN GOGARTY	J. B. Lyons
GEORGE FITZMAURICE	Arthur McGuinness

ELIZABETH BOWEN

Edwin J. Kenney, Jr.

Lewisburg
BUCKNELL UNIVERSITY PRESS
London: ASSOCIATED UNIVERSITY PRESSES

© 1975 by Associated University Presses, Inc.

Associated University Presses, Inc.
Cranbury, New Jersey 08512

Associated University Presses
108 New Bond Street
London W1Y OQX, England

Library of Congress Cataloging in Publication Data

Kenney, Edwin J.
    Elizabeth Bowen.

    (The Irish writers series)
    Bibliography: p.
    1. Bowen, Elizabeth, 1899–1973.
PR6003.06757Z675   823'.9'12   74-168810
ISBN 0-8387-7939-5
ISBN 0-8387-7978-6 (pbk.)

PRINTED IN THE UNITED STATES OF AMERICA

Contents

99810

Acknowledgments

I wish to thank the Humanities Grant Committee of Colby College for a travel and research grant that allowed me to go to Ireland and England and to interview Elizabeth Bowen in the summer of 1971; Nigel Nicolson of Sissinghurst Castle, Kent, for his hospitality and friendship during our stay in England; Jonathan Cape Ltd. of London and Alfred A. Knopf, Inc. of New York for permission to quote from Elizabeth Bowen's fiction and nonfiction; William A. Koshland of Alfred A. Knopf, Inc. for kindly sharing his knowledge of the state of "Pictures and Conversations" and his recollections of his last meeting with Elizabeth Bowen; Professor Douglas N. Archibald, Chairman, Dept. of English, Colby College, for all the illuminating talk about Irish history and literature.

My wife, Susan, deserves special thanks for her patient encouragement and helpful criticism of this essay.

Miss Bowen's gracious kindness to my family and me and her generous cooperation in answering questions, giving permission to quote from her works and to reprint the photograph by Angus McBean receive in memory my warmest gratitude.

9

Chronology

1899   Elizabeth Bowen born in Dublin, Ireland, 7 June.

1906   Her father ill with "anemia of the brain"; goes with mother to England.

1912   Death of mother.

1914-1917 Attends Downe House, Downe, Kent; returns to Ireland to work in hospital for shell-shocked war veterans.

1918   Her father remarried; EB moves to London and attends the London County Council School of Art.

1921   Spends winter at Bordighera.

1923   *Encounters;* marries Alan Charles Cameron, moves with him to Northhampton (1923-25), then to Old Headington, where he worked in the city of Oxford school system; meets C. M. Bowra, Lord David Cecil.

1926   *Ann Lee's.*

1927   *The Hotel.*

1929   *Joining Charles; The Last September.*

1930   At death of father becomes the first female owner of Bowen's Court since its construction in 1776.

1931 *Friends and Relations.*

1932 *To The North.*

1934 *The Cat Jumps.*

1935 *The House in Paris;* moves to Clarence Terrace, Regent's Park, London, where Alan Cameron was employed by the B.B.C.; meets Bloomsbury figures, and reviews for *The Tatler.*

1938 *The Death of the Heart;* stays in London during World War II and works for the Ministry of Information and as air-raid warden.

1941 *Look at All Those Roses.*

1942 *Bowen's Court.*

1943 *Seven Winters.*

1945 *The Demon Lover;* published in the United States as *Ivy Gripped the Steps.*

1946 *English Novelists.*

1948 *Why Do I Write? An Exchange of Views Between Elizabeth Bowen, Graham Greene and V.S. Pritchett;* made a Commander of the British Empire.

1949 *The Heat of the Day;* awarded honory Doctor of Letters, Trinity College, Dublin.

1950 *Collected Impressions.*

1951 *The Shelbourne Hotel.*

1952 Returns to live at Bowen's Court; death of Alan Cameron.

1955 *A World of Love.*

1957 Awarded honory Doctor of Letters, Oxford University.

1960 *A Time in Rome;* sells Bowen's Court and returns to Old Headington, Oxford.

1962 *Afterthoughts.*

1963   Bowen's Court pulled down.

1964   *The Little Girls;* second, revised edition of *Bowen's Court.*

1965   *A Day in the Dark;* moves to Hythe, Kent; made a Companion of Literature.

1969   *Eva Trout.*

1973   After last trip to Ireland, dies in London, 22 February, leaving unfinished an autobiographical manuscript entitled "Pictures and Conversations" to be published with other pieces by Alfred A. Knopf in 1974.

Elizabeth Bowen

I

Elizabeth Bowen was one of the few truly accomplished Irish women novelists and one of the most distinguished writers of her time. But when Elizabeth Bowen died on 22 February 1973, Philip Toynbee accurately pointed out that for "the last 20 years of her life few younger writers paid much attention to her work; she was inescapably of her own time, her own class and her own kind of literary sensibility." The purpose of this brief study is to suggest the nature of Elizabeth Bowen's literary sensibility, how it is, like all sensibilities, "inescapably" of her own time and her own Anglo-Irish experience.

Personal recollections of Elizabeth Bowen are strangely static in their emphasis on the widely traveled and celebrated "writer" in the tradition of Henry James and "the great lady." What struck Elizabeth Bowen's contemporaries was her apparently inherited sense of herself from a "more spacious and more assured society," as C. M. Bowra put it—"her consciousness of who she was and why she was," as Cyril Connolly says. This sense was conveyed by her imposing physical appearance, tall, gaunt, and handsome, and also by her attention to details of social life. She was "smart" in her clothes, elegant in her entertaining, and acerbically witty in her conversation. She is seen permanently in memory as a rather rare creature who, by her presence, heightened one's sense of life.

These poised images of the writer and the great lady were not, however, simply "givens" of Miss Bowen's life; they were, as she felt all life must be, created or recreated "styles," demanding a certain kind of undaunted determination that she ironically calls "hardiness" in her heroines. Only when her friends speak of her refusal to allow her stammer to prevent her from becoming a successful conversationalist, BBC Third Programme broadcaster, and university lecturer does one sense the consciousness of her "command." Beneath these styles, and in the stylishness of Elizabeth Bowen's art, one senses the dislocated child who is urgently seeking an identity as a means of survival, and who sometimes strikes that "kind of *farouche* note which one associates with teen-age delinquents about to break prison—that is, leave home," as her friend Sean O'Faolain said. As Miss Bowen asserts in her most famous novel, *The Death of the Heart,* "Illusions are art. . .and it is by art that we live, if we do." The recurrent theme of Elizabeth Bowen's fiction is man's primary need for an illusion, an image of himself, in order for him to be. Her fascination with problems of identity has its source in the experience of her early life, and it often finds its expression in allusions to the story of the early life of man, the story of the fall from the garden of Eden; for both are stories of the need to be, the loss of innocence, the acquisition of knowledge through loss, and the entrance into selfhood.

In a Preface to her first publication, *Encounters,* written 25 years after the book's initial appearance in 1923, Elizabeth Bowen reveals the feelings that are the source of the creation of her fiction and also her subject:

> Motherless since I was thirteen, I was in and out of the homes of my different relatives—and, as constantly, shuttling between two countries: Ireland and England. I was, it seemed, at everyone's disposition. Though quite happy, I lived with a submerged fear that I might fail to establish grown-up status. That fear, it may be, egged me on to writing: an author, a grown-up, must they not be synonymous? As far as I now see, I must have been anxious to approximate to my elders, yet to demolish them.

The quotation indicates the issues in Miss Bowen's family and cultural life which complicated the adolescent transition from being a child, always kept unknowing and in the power of others, to being an adult with her own autonomy, and which led to her establishing herself as an adult by writing. She was an only child who was alone without a mother or father at critical stages of her development, and she was Anglo-Irish not only by descent but also by physical movement between the two countries at a critical stage in the relations between England and Ireland.

Taken together, these complementary conditions suggest the peculiar ambiguity, tenuousness, and intensity of Elizabeth Bowen's life and work, for to be Anglo-Irish, living on both sides of the hyphen and the water simultaneously separating and joining England and Ireland, means really to be neither more than both. For Miss Bowen, this meant to be always struggling from childhood to become an adult—and from being an only and a female child at that. She showed her own fascination with this background by writing three works of nonfiction specifically about it—*Seven Winters* (1943), "a fragment of autobiography" (it is only 60 pages long) describing her life with her mother and father in Dublin until she was seven; *Bowen's Court* (1942, 1964), a history of her family home, where she spent her summers; and *The Shelbourne Hotel* (1951), a history of the cosmopolitan focus of Anglo-Irish life— and one early novel, *The Last September,* set during the Troubles. The biographical and historical experiences described in these books inform all of Miss Bowen's fiction.

Elizabeth Dorothea Cole Bowen was born 7 June 1899 in Dublin to Henry Cole and Florence Colley Bowen, whose families both shared Anglo-Irish, landowning, Protestant, Unionist views. The Colleys had been in Ireland since the reign of Queen Elizabeth, and the first Bowen, Colonel Henry Bowen, of Gowersland, Glamorganshire, Wales, came over to fight for Cromwell in 1649. For his grim efforts he received land in County Cork, between the Ballyhoura Mountains and the Blackwater, which became the site for Bowen's Court, built by the third Henry Bowen in the eighteenth century, the highpoint of the Protestant Ascendency. The building of Bowen's Court marked the family's decision to live as a part of Ireland but apart from the native Catholic Irish, from whom it was separated by nationality, religion, position, and finally by symbolic and protective walls.

This place defined Elizabeth Bowen's emotional and imaginative connection to Ireland, as it had done for all her family. Her sense of Ireland was not a literary or intellectual one of revived myths and celebrated national heroes; Ireland always existed for her literally in the land itself and in the image of Bowen's Court, behind its demesne walls, at the end of a long avenue, set on the land in its circle of trees. She grew up, as she says of other children of the Big House, *"farouche,* haughty, quite ignorant of the outside world." Her parents' love of their own sphere meant that even in Dublin, where her father was a barrister, they associated only with a small circle of Anglo-Irish friends from the Bar, Trinity College, the Church of Ireland, and "landed people living quietly in town." Elizabeth was not even read Irish fairy tales as a child, and she knew nothing of the Irish Literary Revival until 1916, when she was at school in England and her father's regiment was fired upon and one of his friends killed. That it was not considered important enough as a nationalistic movement for Unionists "to know about or be mad about" indicates the remove at which her family and their group lived from a felt sense of contemporary Irish life—even granting the historical judgment that the significance of the Revival and the Easter Uprising was in their aftermath. The life she led as a child was, as she admitted later, anachronistic. The sense of the past she felt was a social one focused primarily on Anglo-Irish landowning Big House life.

By the time Elizabeth Bowen wrote *Bowen's Court,* after the events of 1916, the Troubles, and the Civil War, which all threatened the existence of Bowen's Court, she had come to an awareness of the severe limitations of this life and the assumptions that lay behind it, an awareness she probably approached even as a child. Significantly she used her own childhood as a simile to describe this life:

> Each of these houses, with its intense, centripetal life, is isolated by something very much more lasting than the physical fact of space; the isolation is innate; it is an affair of origin. It is possible that Anglo-Irish people, like only children, do not know how much they miss. Their existences, like those of only children, are singular, independent and secretive.

This analogy of the only child is not only explanatory; it is also, by extension, apologetic, and somewhat inaccurate. Writing *Bowen's Court* was not entirely easy or pleasant for Miss Bowen, for she had to face up to the guilt that lies at the center of this centripetal life, and she did: "The stretches of the past I have had to cover have been, on the whole painful: my family got their position and drew their power from a situation that shows an inherent wrong." By calling the Anglo-Irish only children she accounts for their imperiousness and cruelty: "perhaps children are sterner than grown-up people in their refusal to suffer, in their refusal, even, to feel at all." Such a view, if it is inaccurate about children, is certainly in accord with her judgment that "The new ascendency lacked feeling; in fact feeling would have been fatal to it," that " the structure of the great Anglo-Irish society was raised over a country in martyrdom. To enjoy prosperity one had to exclude feeling, or keep it within prescribed bounds." By considering the Anglo-Irish as children, one may more easily forgive, or at least accept, them.

So, Miss Bowen characteristically did not dwell on

this Anglo-Irish guilt; she accepted it as almost a given, and she emphasized those acts of good will and good intentions that "have not been allowed by Ireland to stand to the English score." She sympathized with those Anglo-Irish who sincerely wished what they thought best for Ireland without ever fully understanding their alienation from most of Irish life. "If Ireland did not accept them, they did not know it—and it is in that unawareness of final rejection, unawareness of being looked out at from some secretive, opposed life, that the Anglo-Irish naive dignity and, even, tragedy seems to me to stand. Themselves they felt Irish, and acted as Irishmen." This was enough for Elizabeth Bowen, who wished "not to drag up the past but to help lay it," and who, in her own Anglo-Irish, only-child way, felt Irish and thought of herself as an Irish woman and yet tried not to feel too much. But she sensed, as this observation attests, her distance from that "opposed" Irish life.

The phrase "that unawareness of final rejection" suggests betrayal. Miss Bowen's whole conception of the Anglo-Irish naive dignity and tragedy implies and depends on a sense of betrayal, a feeling that the best intentions of the best of her class were somehow betrayed both by others of that class and by the native Irish (as in 1916). This view of the Anglo-Irish in Ireland is also Elizabeth Bowen's view of having been brought up to be Anglo-Irish, and ultimately her view of life itself. In 1937, speaking of her whole generation, she remarked that their lives had changed "inconceivably since childhood. Tradition is broken. Temperament, occupation, success or failure, marriage, or active nervous hostility to an original *milieu* have made nomads of us. The rules we learnt in childhood are as useless, as impossible to take with us, as the immutable furniture of the family home."

The simile of the furniture from the family home shows that Miss Bowen is generalizing from her own experience; this does not invalidate the truth of the generalization—indeed, accounts of others of Miss Bowen's generation who survived The Great War corroborate it. But it does reveal the feeling that she was betrayed by the entire idea and style of life to which she was brought up. The experience of unknowing separation from vital goings-on that is most often violated by a sudden knowledge of betrayal fraught with tragic consequences is what Miss Bowen sees in the history of her class in Ireland and in her being brought up to the expectations of that class at the time she was. This is what she describes as child-like; this is what she felt made her a "nomad" in her travels between Ireland and England, and this is, not surprisingly, the story of her relations with her mother and father, both of whom seemed to abandon and at the same time to implicate her.

To begin with, Elizabeth was supposed to have been born Robert Bowen, a boy, a male heir named after her grandfather; then her parents expected a Robert to follow, but none did, and her mother nearly died trying to bear another child in 1904. Her mother was a beautiful, impractical, strange and remote woman, who must have been so uncertain of herself that she "moved some way away from things and people she loved as though to convince herself that they did exist." From the beginning of her relations with her daughter she was unable to create a sense of trust in the child. Although Elizabeth did not see much of her father because he spent most of his time at the Law Library and his practice, she evidently was able to feel close to him. But at just that time when the attraction of a young girl to her father becomes intensified, Elizabeth Bowen's father seemed to abandon her. When Elizabeth was five, her mother became dangerously ill attempting to bear the expected "Robert," and at this time Henry Cole Bowen began to break down. In the winter of 1905-6 he went to England to be treated, but upon his return he became worse, and Elizabeth and her mother were sent to England, suddenly: "Late one night, after a day of alarms, I was got out of bed by Miss M—; a cab came around and she and I drove through the dark. . . I had left Herbert Place forever, *without knowing.*"*

Although Miss Bowen did not express this connection, it seems clear that her father's first breakdown was somehow related to her mother's illness and the loss of Robert. In 1904, he had failed to give new life to the dead Robert, his father, in the birth of Robert, his son, and he had almost killed his own wife trying. His breakdowns at this time and later in 1928 were directly related to Bowen's Court and through it to his responsibility for his family's suffering. As a young man of nineteen he ignored his father's warning to avoid a smallpox epidemic in London, and, by so doing, brought death to his mother and madness, in both senses of the word, to his father. Such a past explains why Bowen's Court and its preservation and manage-

---

* Italics E. J. K.

ment became such a dangerous obsession with Henry Cole Bowen. Again, although she did not state the connection, Elizabeth Bowen pointed out that "Bowen's Court was the abiding thing in his life—for Henry VI's feeling for Bowen's Court I can find no word that he would have countenanced." In her father's compulsive struggle with Bowen's Court, Elizabeth may have first sensed the wrongs of the past avenging themselves through the very symbol of family and class that epitomized the Ascendency, and perhaps she wondered if she could ever escape this curse as long as she alone was to inherit the responsibility, literally the debts of Bowen's Court. Later she said that "the dead do not need to visit Bowen's Court rooms. . .because they already permeate them."

To prevent just such thoughts she was quickly and mysteriously taken away from her father and her home and sent to England with her governess and mother. In this first breaking up of the insularity of her childhood, Elizabeth's aloneness and insecurity may have been complicated by actual feelings of betrayal, betrayal by her father when she needed him most, betrayal by her mother for taking her away from her father, betrayal by the whole adult conspiracy of governess, doctors, lawyers, and family advisors. Such a feeling would be compounded because she was lied to about these events, and she came to know she was being lied to, which set up the emotionally contradictory but more logical feeling of guilt for these betrayals: by not knowing what the truth is, the child acts in a way that after the event leads her to think that she caused it, that it was a kind of punishment for something she said or did or failed to say or do.

This experience was repeated with her mother in England. Despite Florence Colley Bowen's temperamental remoteness, Elizabeth now became more intimate with her and dependent upon her; there was no longer the interposition of a governess to separate them, and, in their anxious waiting and moving—in a few years they were not only in and out of the homes of relatives, but also they moved along the Kentish coast from Folkstone, to Hythe, to Lyminge, and then back to Hythe—Mrs. Bowen became, whether she liked it or not, Elizabeth's only sense of continuity and security in the midst of all this disruption and uncertainty. These circumstances of Elizabeth's being in England also tended to increase her awareness of distance as "Irish" from the English; since her family had been in Ireland, no Bowen child had ever lived or been educated in England. Elizabeth, an alien further alienated by her suffering and a bad stammer, went to school with a tendency to show off her Irishness, "counterposed by [a] wish to out-English the English by being impossibly fashionable and correct." Thus she felt early what she later called the "Anglo-Irish ambivalence to all things English, a blend of impatience and evasiveness, a reluctance to be pinned down to a relationship." The only central point in this ambivalence was her mother, and this, in turn, led to another and severer shock to her world.

Although Henry Cole Bowen recovered, Elizabeth was not to return to Ireland to live; she remained in England with her mother and her father visited them. She suspected something was wrong, probably because the first of her mother's operations was concealed from her, but she did not know that her mother had cancer.

"The sense of impermanence shifted through to me and made me enjoy our present with an intensity too conscious to be natural in a child. . . .In front of me my mother and father talked plans—plans they came to know to be fictions. . . ." Elizabeth, sensing the impermanence, felt the lie. After two months of continuous pain that could not be concealed from her child, Florence Colley Bowen died, and again the process of betrayal and guilt asserted itself in Elizabeth: if she felt betrayed and abandoned by her mother, she also felt somehow guilty for her death. The cultural experience of the Anglo-Irish and Miss Bowen's family experiences have in common this sense of betrayal and guilt in her feeling of insecurity. What she saw and lived and depended on was a lie, a lie told to her by adults, but a lie for which she felt responsible both for its persistence through her ignorant and tacit assent and for its revelation and dissolution through her resentment and demanding behavior. Especially after the war, this awareness of adults lying about the way things are is what made Elizabeth Bowen believe that she could, or even had to, establish her identity as a grown-up by writing.

Elizabeth learned to read at the age of seven (she was not permitted to learn any earlier by her mother), just that time in her childhood when her family catastrophes began to enter her consciousness with her removal to England. As she said later, "All susceptibility belongs to the age of magic, the Eden where fact and fiction were the same; the imaginative writer was the imaginative child, who relied for life upon being lied to. . . ." Despite her mother's doubts, she saw her early youth, then, as an Eden that cohered and could be trusted; when the lies told to her by her parents and other adults began to be revealed for what they were in her father's breakdown, her mother's cancer and death, and her dislocation, she discovered another kind of lying, that of fiction, to rely on. From this time on, she says, "Nothing made full sense to me that was not in print.... Feeling what a book could do, and what indeed only a book *could* do, made me wish to write: I conceived of nothing else as worth doing." There is a certain fanatical desperation in this commitment, but it worked for Elizabeth Bowen by allowing her to establish a kind of legitimate lying that in itself was not capable of betrayal: whatever happens in a book, however horrible it may be—and Dickens' novels of suffering children, especially *David Copperfield,* were among her favorites—it does not change radically and suddenly on one; it is and remains known, which life does not. The desire to move from participating in such a world as a reader, and an omnivorous one, to becoming a writer, especially in these circumstances, is natural and understandable because to do so is to draw closer the connection of the self and the uncertain actualities of one's own life to the fuller more coherent world of fiction.

The great difference, practical, emotional, and moral, between being lied to and lying oneself is what constitutes the loss of innocence and the achievement of adulthood along with the creation of art. Elizabeth Bowen's memory of suffering at the lies of adults in her childhood makes her especially conscious of the guilt she incurs simultaneously with her feelings of maturation and achievement in writing. All through her creative writing, she confesses, there runs "a sense of dishonesty and of debt." The adult, the writer, like the child, relies for life upon being lied to, but the adult also tells the lies, creates his own fictions for life. The feelings of betrayal and guilt are connected in a circular process in which Miss Bowen recalled and used her feelings of childhood in her creative act as an adult. This circularity manifested itself also in her lifetime of continual "shuttling between Ireland and England" as she did as an Anglo-Irish child. It kept her moving, but in a circumscribed orbit that delineated her psychic distance from both countries and her vacillation between betrayal and guilt. It expressed her feeling, which she attributed to all complex people, of "never being certain that they are not crooks, never certain their passports are quite in order" and of being "unnerved by the slightest thing." This ambivalence about herself, her past, Ireland, England, life, and art defines her literary sensibility as an Anglo-Irish writer. It is resolved by style in fictions for both life and art.

In 1923 Elizabeth Bowen signified her adulthood by publishing her first writing of any kind, the collection of short stories called *Encounters,* and by marrying Alan C. Cameron, an educator. She sought in *Encounters* to "cry out for affirmation" and hoped to find in its publication "the sign that she was not mad." Her work and her home gave her literally and figuratively a new place, which she called a "centre." She was then "not only a writer but married, a matron, the mistress of a house. The sensation of actually *living* anywhere, as apart from camping or visiting," she said, was "new" to her, and obviously comforting and inspiring. In a later

Preface to her second collection of short stories, *Ann Lee's,* she claimed that this new security and confidence made her able "to look back painlessly" at her own past. But the stories of childhood in these first two collections are filled with pain and cannot have been painless to write; two stories are especially vivid in their representation of childhood fear and sorrow: "Coming Home," about a girl living alone with her mother after her father's death, now afraid she has killed her mother by trying to be independent of her; and "The Visitor," about a boy who has been sent to stay with old maiden friends while his mother is dying and who knows more than the adults will tell him but not enough to understand. The experience of the children is Elizabeth Bowen's own: insecurity, loneliness, deception.

It was not, however, until *The Hotel* (1927) and *The Last September* (1929) that she was able or willing to look back to the immediate past of her adolescence and her fears of establishing a grown-up identity. In *The Last September,* Miss Bowen's first important novel, she deals directly with the crisis of being Anglo-Irish at a time of national crisis, called the Troubles. Just as her early stories were written about her childhood at the time of her transition to adulthood, this work, too, marks another stage of transition in her life. She began writing *The Last September* in 1928, the year her father retired from the Bar to take up the life of the County Cork gentleman, master of Bowen's Court, that he had earlier rejected in spite of, or to spite, his father. He had finished his great work, *Statutory Land Purchase in Ireland,* which as a standard work of reference had been outdated before its publication by the Treaty of 1921.

His inactivity permitted him to worry full time about maintaining Bowen's Court; his health soon gave way, and the "illness of mind" that had troubled him in Elizabeth's childhood returned. He died in May 1930, the year after the publication of *The Last September.* The novel, then, may be considered as Miss Bowen's covert way of preparing herself for inheriting Bowen's Court, whose troublesome care, along with her books, would form the chief responsibilities of her adult life.

The achievement of this novel, greater than that of *The Hotel,* is the complementarity it creates between the adolescent crisis of its heroine, Lois Farquar, an orphan in Danielstown, the Big House of her aunt and uncle Naylor, and the cultural and political crisis of the Anglo-Irish in 1920. The Anglo-Irish are seen now as being not just only children but adolescent only children. The suspension between being English and Irish finds its complement in the suspension between being a child and being an adult because this is the time when one feels it most confusedly, as Elizabeth Bowen herself did. Miss Bowen said that this novel was of all her books the one "nearest her heart" and that it had a "deep, unclouded spontaneous source" in her own experience. In the novel, Lois, who had finished school at the end of World War I, is back at Danielstown asking herself the same questions Elizabeth Bowen had: "I asked my self *what* I should be, and when?" Her primary feeling is one of isolation and exclusion from life; she is alone and lonely because she has no close family and no way to define herself or establish meaningful relations with others. She distrusts and is bored by those deliberate "interests," such as drawing, music, or an organization of some kind, considered appropriate to young ladies of her class.

Her only satisfaction is the rather perverse one of deception in fulfilling adult conceptions of what her youth ought to be like. Her "theatrical" role-playing of the "very happy and reckless" young woman to please and complete others, rather than herself, makes her, however, understand and desire a genuine function of her own. It leads her to feel the need for form and pattern that intensifies her sense of self: " 'I like to be in a pattern,' she says, 'I like to be related; to have to be what I am. Just to *be* is so intransitive, so lonely.' " But on the other hand, she has also felt her conscious role–playing to be a restriction and a lie, and she fears the completion of a pattern in her life: "She didn't want to know what she was, she couldn't bear it: knowledge of this would stop, seal, finish one." So Lois remains suspended, incomplete, longing, and fearful. She is able to remain in this state for a prolonged period because she is sustained in it by the style of life at Danielstown, with its ritual of daily existence, and by the Anglo-Irish adults who live there, fulfilling and sustaining Danielstown and mirroring Lois in a state of protected adolescence.

Just as Lois stays at Danielstown because she does not feel there is anyplace or anything or anyone to which she should go, so her aunt and uncle in their ambivalence cling to the demands of host and hostess. Although they appear independent, in their own way they are dependent for their existence on others and they resent it, as adolescents do. The Anglo-Irish of the Big House are dependent on the good will of the local

Irish not to be threatened or destroyed; when they are threatened, they are dependent on the protection of the British. The Anglo-Irish, thus, have no real side during the Troubles; they too are isolated and scared, and they are unable to conceive of another identity for themselves or, if they could, the autonomy to achieve it. "Will there ever be anything we can all do except not notice?" "Not noticing," although it may be the habitual reaction of the Anglo-Irish since they moved in and raised themselves over a country in martyrdom, is not easily done during such times as 1920. But in the caring for Irish tenants, on the one hand, and the entertainment of British soldiers on the other, the management of the farms, and the arrangement of meals and outings for guests, it can be done. The guilty void at the center of such a life can be maintained—even augmented and elaborated—but all at some psychic cost.

This is what constitutes the fundamental affinity Lois, at this time in her life, feels with these people and this place: "after every return—or awakening, even, from sleep or preoccupation—she and these home surroundings still further penetrated each other mutually in the discovery of a lack." The lack is of any vital connection to life, especially to the life of the country; Lois cannot "conceive of her country emotionally." The violent reality of Irish life seems only to exaggerate her sense of being "in some kind of cocoon." To be more moved or involved in the national struggle around her Lois would have to be more complete herself; Elizabeth Bowen underscored this point in her Preface to the American edition of *The Last September:*

This was a creature still half-awake, the soul not yet open, nor yet the eyes. And world war had shadowed her schooldays; *that* was enough—now she wanted order. Trying enough it is to have to grow up, more so to grow up at a trying time. Her generation, mine, put out few rebels and fewer zealots. Like it or not, however, she acquiesced to strife, abnormalities and danger. . . .Tragedy, she could only touch at the margin. . . .

The tragedy that touches Lois's life at the margins comes in the form of the murder of a British officer who loved her but whom she could not love any more than she could love her country, and in the destruction of Danielstown, the illusory sanctuary for her and the Anglo-Irish of the novel. Tragedy cannot, finally, be entirely avoided by innocence or deliberate ignorance, for it is to Elizabeth Bowen the condition of life; but Lois can touch tragedy only at the margins because she is only at the margins of life. If Lois at this point cannot be a participant in tragedy, she can at least be shocked into being a feeling spectator, and from this imaginative experience of life seen as a pattern of tragedy she can learn what all the young people in Elizabeth Bowen's fiction learn, that there is no security, that security and happiness are a game played by grown-ups, that "life, seen whole for a moment, was an act of apprehension of death." One does not know for sure, because Lois is sent off on a tour for her French, but the implication of the novel is that such an experience can, as Shelley argued, exercise her moral imagination and also her courage. This should save her from the fate of the older Anglo-Irish in the novel who should have known better than she, who should have known what the narrative and the narrator Elizabeth Bowen, adult and artist assert: one cannot avoid danger by pretending it is not there, one cannot avoid love by refusing a sexual identity, one cannot avoid commitment by attempting to be uncommitted, one cannot avoid death by refusing to grow up. Elizabeth Bowen the novelist knows, and her knowledge is what makes her the grown-up in her books about children and adolescents.

This maturity was achieved and expressed in Miss Bowen's decision to burn Bowen's Court in imagination at the time she was about to inherit it. Certainly this act can be understood on aesthetic grounds, for the burning of Danielstown in the novel functions to shock Lois into some adult awareness of existential risk and anxiety and to liberate her to accept them. Historically, too, this act can be understood, for many Anglo-Irish Big Houses were burned during the Troubles. In fact, three houses in the immediate neighborhood of Bowen's Court were burned, and their burning forced Elizabeth to experience imaginatively and emotionally the burning of Bowen's Court when she was in Italy during her self-imposed moratorium of 1921. When the three houses nearby were burned, her father wrote to her, warning her to prepare herself for the inevitable:

> I read his letter beside Lake Como, and, looking at the blue water, taught myself to imagine Bowen's Court in flames. Perhaps that moment disinfected the future: realities of war I have seen since have been frightful: none of them have taken me by surprise.

Bowen's Court was not burned down; it survived the destruction of the Troubles and later the Civil War, when it was occupied by Republican forces and mined for explosion. But the image of it burning in Lake Como remained with Elizabeth Bowen: "so often did I see it burning that the terrible last event in *The Last September* is more real than anything I have lived through." This was the risk Miss Bowen had to accept with her inheritance of the house, the burden of its preservation, and the no less real burdens of its inherited guilt. Bowen's Court again reasserted the bipolarity of her life by recalling her from the new "centre" for her life she had created on the other side of the water in her writing and her marriage and home with Alan Cameron, and by recalling her family and cultural past represented in the symbolic structure of the house, whose past associations were tinged by guilt and whose present was without useful function.

Elizabeth Bowen is the adult author-narrator in her novels, and she is also still the Anglo-Irish only child, for one grows up but one does not after all outgrow being an only child. Sometimes one senses in her attitudes about her art the feeling that the world of her writing is a new demesne where she can be again, as her ancestors had been, a rather detached, preoccupied Anglo-Irish landlord, where she can make patterns of her adolescent crises for her lonely characters. To go back even further, it is a return to that Eden where fact and fiction are the same, perfect and clear as a bubble Lois imagines for herself as an alternative to her suffering: "She shut her eyes and tried—as sometimes when she was seasick, locked in misery between Holyhead and Kingstown—to be enclosed in a nonentity, in some ideal no-place perfect and clear as a bubble. . . ." Miss Bowen reduced the risk of being betrayed by being what she called "unsociable"; she expressed this attitude in her

insistence that her writing was her only relation to
society. "Solitary and *farouche* people don't have
relationships: they are quite unrelatable. . . .My writing,
I am prepared to think, may be a substitute for
something I have been born without—a so-called normal
relation to society. My books *are* my relation to
society." She adamantly refused to commit herself
publically on public issues: "My view is that writers
should keep out of pulpits and off platforms, and just
write. They should not for a moment consider putting
their names to petitions or letters to newspapers on
matters that they do not know much about and have no
reason to know anything about." (The only political
article she wrote was characteristically on Ireland's
neutrality during World War II.)

Miss Bowen seems to have dealt with, if not resolved,
her identity confusion by remaining between being
Anglo and Irish, only child and grown-up in a form of
accommodation achieved in her role as writer. Elizabeth
Bowen the novelist was the only adult Elizabeth the
only child could trust. As an adult she knew she was
lying, and as a child she knew she was being lied to, but
the needs of both were fulfilled in the fiction, as before
she and her parents had accepted the fictions of their
future while her mother was dying of cancer and they
all knew it, and as the Anglo-Irish landlords accepted
the fiction of the eternality of their country-house
world while it was being threatened from all sides. If,
especially after the experience of World War II, the
death of her husband at Bowen's Court in 1952, and the
loss and final destruction of Bowen's Court itself in
1960-63, life came to mean—as it does for one of her

child characters—"waiting for something awful to happen and trying to think of something else"; and if her life as a writer was all a lie, a precarious bubble world for a lonely child sick midway between Holyhead and Kingstown, it was a life and a lie that allowed her to say with characteristic toughness and candor, "it is not only our fate but our business to lose innocence, and once we have lost that it is futile to attempt a picnic in Eden." Her limitations were her strengths; she could and did act as though she believed in her own illusions because she had to, but she also knew and accepted them for exactly what they were. This was the achievement of her life and art.

II

Our loss of innocence is the business of Elizabeth Bowen's fiction. Her novels create, obsessively, a sense of insecurity. One is made to feel that life itself cannot be trusted; those we love are taken away by obscure, arbitrary forces such as death, or they betray us. The experience of Miss Bowen's fiction is similar to her description of the experience of Ireland: it tends to drive one "back on oneself."

If our fate is unavoidable and our attempts to picnic in Eden futile, we must make do with our own earth. This is Adam's curse and Elizabeth Bowen's tough-minded admonition. In her novels she is therefore as much or more concerned with the self's response to the experience of loss as she is with the loss itself. Like her admired friends E. M. Forster and Virginia Woolf, she regarded the surface of life as a fragile crust saving us from the bottomless abyss below, and she said that "the more the surface seems to heave or threaten to crack, the more its actual pattern fascinates me." Once "the crack appears across the crust of life," Miss Bowen is concerned with how her characters work around it, for ultimately there is no making the crack go away or pretending it is not there. If one tries not to acknowledge it, one risks self-destruction; one falls into the abyss. This horrible alternative to creating a new pattern that includes the knowledge of life's evils is explored in *To The North.*

Neither *To The North* (1932) nor Miss Bowen's preceding novel, *Friends and Relations* (1931), should be ranked among her best works. Despite moments of fine writing and comic effect, both are rather static books with diagrammatic design the execution of which seems to have squeezed the life out of them. In *To The North* this design is that of melodramatic tragedy: an innocent girl, Emmeline—relentlessly called an angel—is seduced and betrayed by a satanic villain, Markie; she subsequently brings about both their deaths, ironically becoming an angel of death. Elizabeth Bowen underscores this archetypal inevitability in the novel:

> Here are no guarantees. Tragedy is the precedent: Tragedy confounding life with its masterful disproportion. . . . . Innocence walks with violence; violence is innocent, cold as fate; between the mistress's kiss and the blade's is a hair-breadth only, and no disparity; every door leads to death. . . .The curtain comes down, the book closes—but who is to say that this is not so?

Unlike Lois in *The Last September,* Emmeline is thus at the center of the tragic action, and her capacity for feeling places her there. This quality is part of her innocence and her fatality because she does not see the dangers, within and without, that threaten her. She is characterized as nearsighted and, although she requires glasses, she chooses not to wear them on social occasions, times of most perilous encounters.

What makes Emmeline transcend the archetypal innocent is the way Elizabeth Bowen shows how Emmeline has coped with her situation though her disability goes unrecognized by all those around her. Emmeline is unlike Miss Bowen's other heroines who have nothing to do, or who have only those "deliberate interests" for young ladies that provide excuses for luncheons. Emmeline, an orphan who lives with her widowed sister-in-law Cecilia in St. John's Wood, owns and manages a successful travel agency with a partner. Because she has created this busy life for herself, Emmeline appears to Cecilia and her Aunt Georgina Waters as entirely independent and capable, and, in retrospect, she seems to have been that way since she was orphaned at the age of twelve. But Emmeline's apparent engagement in life, in the expectations and travels of others, and especially in facts, such as the exact departure times of trains and rates of exchange, is both an illusory compensation and a mask for her self-contained withdrawal from life. Her life with Cecilia in their just-right house and her life as a "career girl" are fictions that inadequately express herself. The older and wiser, if duller, Cecilia, who has had to cope with the loss of her husband, sees that she knows nothing of Emmeline, even though she lives with her: "she lent herself to a fiction in which she did not believe; for she lived with nobody." But Emmeline is unable to discern the fictive nature of the life she has made for herself, and she is consequently unable to discern its inadequacies or precariousness.

Only at certain moments are Emmeline's desires for perfection beyond the ordinary demands of time and space clearly felt although still not understood by her. At Lady Waters's country house, rather cutely named Farraways, Emmeline, anticipating another busy Monday at her agency, feels that place "like some image of childhood, unaccountably dear but remote." Efficiently driving her car, she recreates in actual perception that "blurred repetitive pattern she took to be life"; and flying in an airplane "some quite new plan of life, forgotten between flight and flight" seems to reveal itself to her. Emmeline's immersion in the business of movement, the agent and sign of change, is actually her unconscious way of distancing herself from change and thus apparently "fixing" it, making it appear stable through her own control. Emmeline, the orphan, the dislocated child, is characterized by Miss Bowen as "the stepchild of her uneasy century." This is Elizabeth Bowen's vision of herself, and Emmeline's attraction to travel, like Miss Bowen's, is an expression of this dislocation and an attempt at accommodation with the condition of it. As Miss Bowen put it in her "travel book," *A Time in Rome,* "I shrink from the feeling of being foreign—who does not? Mine may be a generation with an extra wish to acclimatize, to identify. Any-where, at any time, with anyone, one may be seized by the suspicion of being alien—ease is therefore to be found in a place which nominally *is* foreign: this shifts the weight." Emmeline finds some ease in the activity of travel as the nominal condition of being dislocated and being alien, but her most intensely felt desire, like Miss Bowen's, is for permanence.

Emmeline is led to seek this permanence in Markie because he is the "natural offspring" of their dislocated century and therefore is at home in it. He appears to satisfy Emmeline's longings for a home that is here and real, but with the idealized perfection of the "far away." Emmeline's "entirety of surrender" to Markie is really her "entire wish" to achieve stability and identity. This is why it is so disturbing to Markie, who, as the natural offspring of dislocation, has eliminated the desire for stability from his expectations for life; he must therefore betray Emmeline's commitment to him.

The effect of Emmeline's commitment and Markie's betrayal follows Elizabeth Bowen's vision of human experience exactly. As soon as Emmeline gives herself to Markie, she feels a sense of infidelity and guilt toward her life with Cecilia. Having violated the limitations of this fiction by admitting Markie, Emmeline has lost her only sanctuary, which at the moment and because of her loss she now sees as an Eden. With Markie's abandonment of her, first emotional then actual, she is overcome with "a sense of being swept strongly apart on a current from all she had held to" and with a corresponding sense of physical disintegration.

> Timber by timber [the house in St. John's Wood] fell to bits, as small houses are broken up daily to widen the road of London. She saw the door open on emptiness: blanched walls as though after a fire. Houses shared with women are built on sand. She thought: 'My home, my home.'

Having lost her "innocence," Emmeline does not yet know that it is futile to attempt to picnic in Eden, and even if she did, it is unlikely that she would be able to imagine what else there was for her to do. So in returning to her lost "home," she exaggerates her sense of dislocation to the point of psychic disintegration.

"Broken up like a puzzle the glittering summer lay scattered over her mind, cut into shapes of pain that had no other character." After a dinner party to which Cecilia and her new fiance'Julian have invited Markie, in the mistaken notion that he and Emmeline are still friends, Emmeline drives Markie to Baldock and is entirely overcome by her sense of being swept apart on a current. At this moment, Emmeline, all her fictive images for herself destroyed in her relation to Markie, feels herself to be no one, and this sensation is the immediate cause of her loss of self and actual loss of life. "She was lost to her own identity, a confining husk." In powerful, moving prose, Elizabeth Bowen describes Emmeline turning "to the north" and her own death as pure force, not consciously seeking suicide or vengeance, but "driven" by the abstract, inhuman powers of time and space, recorded in Markie's horrified stare at the clock and speedometer. No longer having anything left "to hold on to," she submits to the strong current.

Emmeline and Markie, killed in the automobile crash, are survived by the passionless and prudent Cecilia and Julian. Emmeline's desperate, romantic innocence is survived by Cecilia's conventional social wisdom. This wisdom, although located in essentially unattractive characters, is not, however, denigrated by Elizabeth Bowen. On the contrary, she sees heroic courage in Cecilia's ability to face the pain of her first husband's loss and the risk of her new marriage to Julian. As Emmeline sees too late, "one does oneself in"; the century may be dislocated, and one may be surrounded by extremely disabled companions, but one is responsible for creating one's own life nevertheless. Cecilia makes up what she has lost in feeling by her understanding of this fundamental truth. It is of her only that Miss Bowen can say, "Obstinate in its refusal to suffer, the spirit puts up defenses; the frightened heart repairs itself in small ways. Very few remain ennobled; one has to live how one can. . .." From Elizabeth Bowen this is high praise. Cecilia, in her limited but courageous way, chooses to live however she can by relocating herself within an acceptable fiction, something to hold on to against the flux.

The importance of fictive concords to overcome the fragmentariness of life and the self is nowhere more poignantly expressed by Miss Bowen than in the disjointed *The House in Paris* (1935). This novel is about a mother's failure to reunite herself with her child because of her lack of imagination and courage; she desires this union to unify herself, to connect her past with the boy's present in a new future for them both, but she is afraid to accept the risk of failure. As in *The Hotel* and *The Last September*, Miss Bowen uses the architectural framework of the house in Paris as a structure for her fiction, an enclosure for her characters, and an emblem of their lives. But this novel is distinguished by her use of the child as a vantage point for viewing the conduct of the adults and by her bold division of the book into three sections that juxtapose time in such a way as to express the separation between child and adult. Part I, "The Present," describes the first part of the child's day up until he learns that his mother will not come to meet him; Part II presents his mother's past; and Part III, also in the present day, describes the child's meeting with his stepfather, who does come to get him.

The child's loneliness, often caused by deaths or separation of parents or abandonment by them, is for Elizabeth Bowen a metaphor for all human loneliness caused by the combination of fate, of external circumstances, and innocence. The child is alone because he does not know what is going on outside of and often within himself; in this sense the child is an outsider to any family, community, or place, whose tacit organization, conduct, and values he does not understand. In this same sense we are all outsiders at times, all children and innocents. This explains why the metaphor of the child can be so easily substituted for or combined with Miss Bowen's other favorite metaphor for her life and the human condition, that of the alien, the traveler. Leopold, the eleven-year-old boy in *The House in Paris,* is an abandoned child who has traveled from the home of his foster parents to the strange house of Mme. Fisher in Paris, where he expects to meet his real mother for the first time. Knowing his mother has sent for him, Leopold comes seeking and expecting his identity; he believes that he will enter joyously into full being when he meets his mother. The house is "narrow," filled with objects that seem somehow "aggressive"; it is a Dickensian place, closed in on itself, as the grip of the deadly Mme. Fisher, who is dying, closes on the lives of those who pass through here. In this foreboding place, witnessed by a bothersome nine-year-old girl on her way to visit her grandmother in Mentone, Leopold must cope with betrayal by his mother and his own weeping for the "end of imagination."

The boy's mother, Karen, cannot achieve what she desires, the child expects, and what the narrator identifies and provides: an act of imaginative connection that is the basis of life and art. "Only. . .in heaven or art, in that nowhere, on that plane—could Karen have told Leopold what had really been." The middle section of the novel, "The Past," is therefore cast in the form of a hypothetical account of what Karen might have said if she actually came to meet Leopold. This section traces the boy's illegitimate origins to his mother's stay in this same house as an adolescent girl years ago. By setting the action of both sections and times in the same house, under the remote and sinister control of the same woman, Miss Bowen shows that the relation of the past and present is reciprocal: the past not only creates and defines the present for these characters, but also the present creates and defines the past. This point is represented in the relation of parent and child, for a child naturally creates and brings up his parents as much as they create and raise the child. The experience of Leopold and his mother and the relation between them is one of searching, unsatisfactory imagination and discovery of the other and, through the other, of the self.

The ideal account of Karen's past explains Karen's inability to meet Leopold by revealing her divided nature. Like Leopold, she once had her own imaginative expectations for life, but she could not integrate them with the values she inherited from her parents. Unlike most of Miss Bowen's heroines, Karen grows up with both parents; they are "good" people, intelligent, open, and secure in their ability to cope. "Up against no one, they are hard to be up against," and this is Karen's trouble; she wants to be up against her parents' world, to be all that it is not. She desires the impulsive, intense, and excessive, but at the same time—in the adolescent, ambivalent way that Miss Bowen felt was characteristic of the Anglo-Irish—Karen also wishes to continue to inhabit this world, for it is comfortable, sensible, and secure. She wants always to be safe but not be to be constrained by safety; she has "enjoyed her mother's anti-romanticism" and at time shares it, but she also wants to be romantic.

Unable to reconcile the contradictory parts of her life, or to eliminate either of them, Karen is unhappily suspended between them in a state of paralysis, and she desperately rushes from one extreme to the other. The extremes are represented by her parents' Regent's Park home and Mme. Fisher's house in Paris, and by her fiancé Ray Forrestier and her lover Max. When as a girl she stays in Mme. Fisher's house, Max, a young protégé of Mme. Fisher's, excites all her adolescent sexuality, but upon her return home she acquiesces to her parents' world and later becomes engaged to marry Ray, a solid, promising diplomat. She tries not to keep asking herself "What next? What Next?", but a visit to her dying aunt in Ireland increases her desperation by making her feel the anxiety of death, "fate is not an eagle, it creeps like a rat." She needs to feel intensely; young girls, the narrator says, "want to suffer...to have loud chords struck on them. Loving art better than life they need men to be actors; only an actor moves them, with his telling smile, undomestic, out of touch with the everyday that they dread."

Max fulfills this need in Karen. As an Anglo-French Jew with no family, no home, and no money, Max is ruthlessly aggressive and calculating; he is, with Mme. Fisher's encouragement and guidance, a man on the make, seeking the "exercise of vulgar power, simply." At the time of Karen's engagement to Ray, Max becomes engaged to Mme. Fisher's daughter, Naomi, whose recent inheritance from an aunt makes her a financially advantageous match for Max—if he can't have family at least he can have some money. But Mme. Fisher has enjoyed in a sensual way her intellectual, social, and willful exploitation of Max's vulnerable rootlessness, and to prevent Max's marriage to Naomi, Mme. Fisher sends Max to London to meet Karen again, then Mme. Fisher tells Max that Karen loves him. Max's opposition to Ray and the world of Karen's parents makes him attractive to her; to love Max would be finally to challenge all the good sense and good conduct of her relations with her parents and to satisfy her growing desire for passion and risk.

Karen's wish to suffer is extended to make others experience her as suffering, to make them suffer. This is why her act of love with Max is felt as a revolutionary act and why she feels disappointed when she thinks that no one will ever know. "One hopes too much of destroying things. If revolutions do not fail, they fail you."

But, as Max says, one cannot simply act; there will be consequences and not simple ones, not ones that can be foreseen or understood. The child Leopold will come from this night of revolutionary action, and he will not be the innocently romantic "mark our hands did not leave on the grass"; he will be "disaster"; and he will *be* despite Karen's later attempts to return to safety by word magic ("No one will ever know. When Naomi came out, the print on the grass was gone. He will never be born to be my enemy"). Leopold is born to be Karen's original wish fulfilled: she suffers and so too does everyone around her; she does not regain the security of Regent's Park as it was before. Her mother dies, as does Max, by his own hand. What Max cannot foresee is that he and Karen were coming to love one another and to wish to marry. Most crucially he cannot see that in choosing to take this "leap in the dark" with Karen, he is in fact not willing his own fate but fulfilling Mme. Fisher's strategy for dominating him. That discovery will destroy everything for him and he will destroy himself.

The significance of the novel's concluding in the present, of the whole experience of Karen and Max being framed by the present life of Leopold, and of the entire life of the novel being framed by the house in Paris is that life is going on and repeating itself. Karen, in reaction to extreme action with Max, secretly abandons Leopold to Naomi and adoptive parents and marries Ray Forrestier after all. She is again seeking safety, although she now knows that nothing can make life safe; she is again desiring the intensity in life that is manifest in Leopold, but she cannot bring herself completely to accept him. She remains caught between the contradictory parts of her own nature. Mme. Fisher, as she made Max "shoot up like a plant enclosed in air," is now seeking to exploit Leopold's "bastard's pride" and "hatred of exile" by convincing him of the power of his own will: "To find oneself like a young tree inside a tomb is to discover the power to crack the tomb and grow up to any height." "Evil" dominates the house in Paris in the sense that people who cannot genuinely make their own lives—children, adolescents, and incomplete adults—will have them determined for them by Mme. Fisher, whom Karen now sees as a "witch," or anyone else whose "outsized will" fulfills itself in love of power over the lives of others and can "overreach" itself in their destruction. If one does not create a pattern for one's own life, one becomes part of someone else's. Although nothing makes life safe, one greatly increases the opportunities for danger by pretending behind a shell of lies that it does not exist ("What has made home such a shell? After all, they were trying to keep me safe"). But, at the same time, the discovery of life's perils must not be permitted to destroy one's power to create and believe in the illusion of safety or one's great expectations for life.

Ironically, it is the "safe" Ray Forrestier, like Cecilia in *To The North,* who represents this wise point of view. When he learns of Karen's failure to meet Leopold, he comes to the house in Paris, and he decides to take Leopold to Karen no matter what the risks. He knows that Leopold must be included in both their lives if they are all to be complete persons, but he also knows that Karen's reaction is uncertain, that of the adoptive parents is going to be injured and outraged, and Leopold is sure to be difficult. Nothing makes life easy, not even in small matters; as Ray says in his initial warnings to Leopold, "There are many things that you will not like. There are many things that I do not like about you."

Ray acts; he does not just react, so he can break the neurotically repetitive and enclosed patterns of life in the house in Paris. He makes a romantic gesture but with anti-romantic clarity about its consequences. Unlike Karen, he raises himself to the level of the child's expectations and possibilities: "The child commanded tonight. I have acted on his scale." That, in this novel, is the best that one can do.

In *The House in Paris* the scale of the child's possibilities really serves only as a frame for the story of Karen's divided self, which takes up the long central section of the novel. This is a flaw in the book, for the attention to Karen detracts from the implied subject of the relations between child and adult. Although one can believe that Karen would not confront her child, one is haunted by Karen's absence in the "present" of the novel. The unsatisfactory nature of Karen's personality and her relation to her child carries over to the structure and effect of the novel. In *The Death of the Heart* (1938), the child becomes not only a focal point for viewing the adults but also the heroine of the novel. This work is the culmination of Elizabeth Bowen's treatment of the theme of youthful innocence confronting the risks of life in a world of unsympathetic, "fallen" adults, the finest of her novels, and a significant achievement in modern fiction. It is a triumph of the "well-made" realistic novel, in which the conception, organization, and realization of each of the parts and characters and their relations to one another and to the settings are in perfect accord. Miss Bowen's own ambivalence is here given its fullest expression in the familiar oppositions between child and adult, innocence and experience, past and present, man and woman.

The Death of the Heart is Elizabeth Bowen's most complete statement of the way the child's expectations and desires must confront and become transformed into the style and art of the adult, and of the way this process at the same time vitalizes and humanizes the artfulness of the adults, saving them from corruption and death. The title of the novel is slightly ambiguous because there is no final death of the heart either in the child or the adults; there is rather a transference of the innocence of heart from the child to the adult and of the restraints of the heart from the adult to the child. There must be, Miss Bowen tells us, a death of our innocence, but we must not lose heart if we are to survive. The adults in their disillusionment and their responses of "style" and "policy" possess what Forster called undeveloped hearts and run the risk of the death of the heart, but they may be saved by the child's innocence, just as the child, facing the inevitable loss of innocence, may be saved by the strategies of the adults.

Portia, the heroine, is the best of all the bad little girls in Miss Bowen's fiction. At age sixteen, after the death first of her father and then her mother, Irene, she is sent to live with her stepbrother and sister-in-law Thomas and Anna Quayne at 2 Windsor Terrace, Regent's Park, to experience what her father thought would be "normal, cheerful, family life." Because Portia was conceived illegitimately during the late years of her father's life, while he was still married to the first Mrs. Quayne, she had always lived abroad and after Mr. Quayne's death traveled with Irene from one out-of-season hotel to another. Her entry into the life of Thomas and Anna is, then, the reentry of the past, which to them is embarrassing, cheap, and vulgar because it was passionate, a quality they by agreement have not sought or achieved in their marriage. The energy of passion and the confidence of mutual trust, because they are not the essence of the Quaynes' marriage, seek their outlet in aggressive isolation and snobbish fantasy. Both Thomas and Anna are prey to their own repressed passions inside their marriage and their fastidiously elegant Regent's Park house.

Anna, betrayed by the one passionate love of her life, marries Thomas on the rebound because he does not demand passion from her and suggests order in his "solid, sub-imperial presence." As an amateur interior decorator, Anna "always thinks how things look," is stylish, and her design for life, including human relations, strives for visual effects of beauty, neatness, poise, rather than full expression of urgent needs. She has surrounded herself with beautiful objects and safe bachelor admirers: St. Quentin, a distant author; Eddie, an irascible young man; Major Brutt, a sturdy mature one. Her hardiness in putting herself back together after her emotional betrayal has now turned into hardness. Thomas, who always dreaded passion, marries Anna because she does not expect it from him, only to discover himself "the prey of a passion for her, inside marriage, that nothing in their language could be allowed to express, that nothing could satisfy." Confined to his business and his study at home, he now no longer cares for life.

It is no wonder that Portia, used to the close, spontaneous, affectionate companionship of her mother, would be puzzled by life at 2 Windsor Terrace and would "create a situation." Portia expects feeling, senses it being deflected and repressed, and wishes to be felt herself. She is confused by the lack of "connection" between what people say and feel and do, and she fears that the fault may be in her. "She could not believe there was not a plan of the whole set-up in every head but her own." But she wants to know what is going on, and she pursues her "research" by recording this new home life in a diary, hoping to make sense of her clues and to put herself in touch with the vital, felt life apprehended in the frenzy underlying the genteel surface—just as she puts together the pieces of puzzle given to her by Major Brutt. But she has difficulty doing all this, for she attracts and includes the other characters in some form of alliance with her and by so doing forces on them self-discoveries which their whole approach to living has been calculated to avoid. In return, they betray her innocent trust in them. The condition of the lives of the adults is stated at the end of the novel by St. Quentin: "I swear that each of us keeps, battened down inside himself, a sort of lunatic giant—impossible socially, but full-scale—and that it's the knockings and batterings we sometimes hear in each other that keeps our intercourse from utter banality."

The lunatic giant is another definition of the innocent, *farouche* child; the restrictive conventions of adult social intercourse cannot fully release the child within, for the child is impossible, as Portia is. She expects feeling, and she expects it to be honestly, directly, and fully expressed and satisfied. If it is not, she demands to know why it is not and insists that it should be. The adults control the impossible child within themselves as they seek to control Portia, but they should be careful not to kill the child; they should care for it and allow it to be heard and seen, occasionally and with some restraint. It is this recognition of the need for limitations that Portia, the complete child, cannot understand, and as the only child in this house full of adults she calls forth the child within them which embarrasses them and whose exposure they resent. This is why, as the narrator says, children and other innocent people are "bound to blunder, then to be told they cheat. . . ." "Incurable strangers to the world, they never cease to exact a heroic happiness. Their singleness, their ruthlessness, their one continuous wish makes them bound to be cruel, and to suffer cruelty."

The three sections of *The Death of the Heart,* marking Portia's disillusionment, are identified by the classical language of the Litany; they explore "the deceits of the world, the flesh, and the devil." In each of these crises Portia suffers cruelty, but never ceases to "exact an heroic happiness" and so she, too, is cruel. This is especially true of her relation to Anna, who is her antithetical double. Portia represents to Anna all of her own childish expectations that she has so painfully locked up but not outgrown; Anna represents to Portia all of the corrupt adult calculating that she must not grow up to accept; and each is constantly being made aware of the other's disapproval. The "system of affections" at Anna's house is "The World" of Part I of the novel. Portia's encounter with Anna's own "troubadour" Eddie with no last name is another one of her blunders and is represented in Part II, "The Flesh."

Anna's St. Quentin, the writer, is "The Devil" of Part III; as the professional liar among the adults, he understands and tells Portia that what she experiences as corruption is simply the adult necessity to live however one can. All of these experiences exacerbate the struggle between Portia and Anna and finally bring them both to recognize the affinity between them.

Portia's attraction to Eddie is based on more than desperation, although there is certainly enough of that in it. He is the most convincing and compelling characterization of a young man in Elizabeth Bowen's works. At twenty-three, he is the only male close to Portia's age whom she meets at the Quaynes, and he is the most dynamic. Unlike the others, he possesses "one of those natures in which underground passion is, at a crisis, stronger than policy," and Portia, always sensitive to passion in this house, senses it directly in him. Because he had had to make his way from nowhere through Oxford and London to Thomas' advertising agency, where he is employed as a bright young man, and has had to be "too much influenced by people's manner towards him," Eddie courts the crises that permit him to reveal his underground passions. Like Portia, with whom he identified ("You and I are the same: we are both rather wicked or rather innocent"), Eddie has blundered in the past by innocently assuming that people meant what they said or suggested. He tried, for example, to make love to Anna because that is what her encouragement of him suggested she desired. So he knows, being older than Portia, enough of the "world" to anticipate the inconsistencies and treacheries of adult strategies for living and to respond with his own.

Finding that he cannot "get on" with people, he instead contrives to "get off" with them by saying and doing outrageous, "impossible" things that break all the "rules" of acceptable drawing room behavior, such as continuing to parody the lover to annoy Anna. If his strategy, like those of the adults in the novel, seems to border on the self-destructive, his conscious conception of it elevates it to the saving status of art. He tells Portia that "we're all full of horrible power, working against each other however much we may love," and he has confidence in the existence of a real Eddie, even if he may be isolated from love. "I may be a crook but I'm not a fake—that is an entirely different thing."

As he did for Anna, Eddie creates "a small world of art round [Portia]," and this binds her to him, for this "poetic order" whirls her "free of a hundred puzzling humiliations, of her hundred failures to take the ordinary clue." This order is that of Eddie's vision of himself as a kind of subversive guerrilla fighter against the world: "Plot—It's a revolution: it's our life. The whole pack are against us. So hide, hide everything." Portia writes in her diary "Eddie says our lives are not our fault," and he becomes her "whole reason to be alive."

Despite the embattled quality of Eddie's vision, Portia's idealistic view of their relation endows it with an isolated, romantic, tranquillity. Portia's view of Eddie excludes passionate relations between man and woman and overlooks Eddie's independence and unreliability. When Portia is forced to discover these aspects of Eddie, she sees them in his attentions to another, so the discovery of passionate sex becomes associated with betrayal and exclusion. This discovery takes place, fittingly, away from 2 Windsor Terrace. When Thomas and Anna seek to escape the pressures of Portia's presence in their house by going to Capri and by having the house thoroughly cleaned in their absence, Portia is sent to stay with Anna's former governess Mrs. Heccomb and her two step-children, Dickie and Daphne, at their home, "Waikiki," in Seale-on-Sea. Compared to the "edited life in the Quaynes' house, " the "unedited-ness of life" at Waikiki makes for "behavior that was pushing and frank. Nothing set itself up here but the naivest propriety. . . ." When at the movies Portia sees Eddie furtively holding hands with Daphne and Daphne responding enthusiastically, she feels that Eddie is in complicity with others against herself, rather than in league with her against others. Her whole reason for living is destroyed, and so too, temporarily, is she.

Portia's "pact with life, a pact of immunity," derived from her vision of her relation to Eddie, is violated; "the peace tears right across." For Elizabeth Bowen, Portia's love—all love—exists only as a widened susceptibility to the threats of life; "it is felt at the price of feeling all human dangers and pains. . . . Pity the selfishness of lovers: it is brief, a forlorn hope; it is impossible." One cannot remain alone, without illusion and love, but every relationship that sustains one's life also exposes it to destruction by betrayal and chaos.

In her desolation at Eddie's betrayal, Portia is again driven back onto herself, and for something to cling to she turns to "imperturbable *things.*" "Pictures would not be hung plumb over the centres of fireplaces or wallpapers pasted on with such precision that their seams make no break in the pattern if life were really not possible to adjudicate for." In their air that nothing has happened these things "remind us how exceedingly seldom the unseemly or unforeseeable rears its head." Portia is coming to feel that life really is impossible to adjudicate for and that its challenge is how to cope; significantly this apprehension is associated with Anna's attention to interior decoration. The perfection of pictures and wallpapering covers the surface of life with art and creates the illusion of security. Portia must learn that "illusions are art, for the feeling person, and it is by art that we live, if we do. It is the emotion to which we remain faithful, after all: we are taught to recover it in some other place." For Elizabeth Bowen this is the fundamental truth about living. But before Portia can consciously appreciate the value of illusion, she must return to 2 Windsor Terrace to be further disillusioned.

Portia must face the "Devil" in the concluding section of the novel to bring her to full consciousness of her experiences in the world and the flesh. When Portia returns to London she is told by St. Quentin that he and Anna have been reading her diary. Although he rather cruelly reveals this betrayal of her, he is "not really sorry" because he believes that this or something like it, "was bound to happen sooner or later" and that he has performed a useful educational service for Portia, who tearfully acknowledges "I suppose it's better to know." St. Quentin, the man of art, is the devil who tells her that she is wrong to keep a diary to get at the facts, the truth, for "there's never such a thing as a bare fact" and that what matters is illusion, the saving lie. What he tells her is what she has felt in herself before and what brings her closer to the adults in the world: "What makes you think us wicked is simply our little way of keeping ourselves going. We must live, though you may not see the necessity."

Although Portia may now see that life demands a conscious effort to live it, she still cannot accept this, so she runs away from the Quaynes', first to Eddie and then to Major Brutt, still hoping to find a safe world elsewhere. Both reject her and the idealistic demands she makes on them. She is innocent, desperate, and ruthless as she offers herself to these men and tries to convince them to commit themselves to her. Not being willing to give up the world or the flesh, Eddie becomes, like St. Quentin, a kind of devil, and he offers, more cruelly, the same advice. He tells Portia to modify her "completely lunatic set of values" because "my God, we've got to live in the world." Portia has the same effect on Major Brutt; by insisting on the innocence he shares with her, she pushes him further into the world. As he tries to deal with her in his practical, 1914-1918, estate manager way, he sees "what a fiction was common-sense," but, faced with this crisis, he strives to retain his hold on this fiction as his personal way of keeping himself going in tenuous touch with the world.

Major Brutt's notion of "the only thing possible to do" in these circumstances is to call the Quaynes and arrange to return Portia to them. At this point, systematically betrayed by all the adults she trusted and having no things to fall back on, Portia performs a final, self-conscious dramatic act and elevates herself to the level of art governing the behavior of the adults. She tells Brutt she will return to the Quaynes only if they do "the right thing." This is the reader's last view of Portia, and it significantly shows her turning toward the "world" of the beginning of the novel, rather than attempting to escape it and the flesh in some dream of spiritual loving in eternal light. But she has not capitulated entirely; she still courageously seeks to make the world live up more closely to her personal demands, to meet her needs. This point of compromise, achieved by a death of the heart's innocence without a complete loss of heart, identifies Portia's essential integrity as a whole person, child and adult, and Elizabeth Bowen's essential response to life. Portia will attempt to picnic in Eden no longer; she will, like Elizabeth Bowen, choose to be both a child and an adult in some form of accommodation.

What assures us that the hearts of the adults in the novel are not dead is that a similar process in reverse seems to be going on at 2 Windsor Terrace. Anna, Portia's enemy, against whom she has struggled ever since her arrival, is the one to decide how to respond to Portia's demand. For the first time she projects herself sympathetically into Portia's place, instead of reacting against her as a threat, and she does this at the risk of revealing her own feelings to Thomas and St. Quentin: "Frantic, frantic desire to be handled with feeling, and, at the same time, to be let alone. Wish to be asked how I felt, great wish to be taken for granted. . .." If she were Portia, she would like to be called for and taken away by someone who would not make any "high class fuss." So they decide to send Matchett, the house-keeper, who came from the home of Mr. Quayne's first wife and has always been affectionate toward Portia.

She understands the difference between "right" actions and "good" ones and appreciates the combination when she sees it. So Matchett is sent to call for Portia and the novel ends with her taxi ride to the hotel and her feeling summer coming to London, and hearing upon her arrival someone playing the piano uncertainly, halting, striking true notes and finding his way to a chord. If, as in the conclusion to *The House in Paris,* this feeling of harmony is justified by adults having met for the first time the expectations of the child aspiring to full selfhood, there is also the same problematic ambivalence of the future surrounding these symbols—just as Adam and Eve after the death of their innocence faced an ambivalent future in the world. Anna's act of sympathy and style saves Portia's dignity and redeems herself, but she knows that her feelings of affinity with Portia also imply differences and difficulties. This knowledge, because it is openly accepted as a necessary starting point, along with Anna and Thomas's other statements of their feelings, justifies the hope suggested by these symbols of fruition and harmony. But Elizabeth Bowen knows hope is only an illusion necessary for life to go on; this is why she never represents actual reconciliation in her novels. She cannot because she does not really believe in its efficacy in solving or illuminating the problems of human life, and she is too honest and tough-minded to say otherwise. As she remarked about the stories in *Ann Lee's,* "Up against human unknowableness, I made that my subject—how many times? The stories are questions posed. . . .I cannot consider these trick endings; more it seemed to me that from true predicament there *is* no way out." We remain faithful to the illusions that sustain life and are its art because we know that as pacts of security and peace they are so suddenly and completely broken. The knockings and batterings we sometimes hear warn us of that.

There are eleven years between the publication of *The Death of The Heart* (1938) and Elizabeth Bowen's next and most ambitious novel, *The Heat of the Day* (1949). During these war years when the private, internal knocking and battering took public, external forms, Miss Bowen stayed in London and worked in the Ministry of Information and as an air-raid warden. She wrote two collections of short stories, *Look at All Those Roses* (1941) and *The Demon Lover* (1945), and her historical and autobiographical *Bowen's Court* (1942) and *Seven Winters* (1943). As it was for everyone, this anguished time was crucial to Miss Bowen, but it was crucial not so much because it was a terrifying shock to the ordinary illusions of security as because it confirmed her earlier experiences, personal and fictional, that there is no security. All of her writing done at this time has a coherence in its repeated emphasis on what she now called fantasy and hallucination, the strongest expression of what had always been Miss Bowen's main subject—illusion. These works, written during and reflecting the most awful happenings, show, in the face of the extremity of actual catastrophe, the instinctive and great power of the human imagination to create and sustain new images of peace and immunity that allow life to go on.

The war was for Elizabeth Bowen a reliving of her earlier traumatic experiences of separation, loss, and terror; it re-created the childhood apprehension that nothing is safe. As she remarks in *Bowen's Court,* "England became for me, when I was seven, the image of every kind of immunity. . . . So much so that now, when I hear bombs fall on England, or see rubble that used to be a safe house, something inside me says '*Even here?*' " The destruction of buildings, places, and things confirmed Miss Bowen's earlier observations of how dependent on things one is for one's sense of self and how the final loss of those familiar things forces one to recover elsewhere one's sense of continuous identity:

> People whose homes had been blown up went to infinite lengths to assemble bits of themselves—broken ornaments, odd shoes, torn scraps of the curtains that had hung in a room—from the wreckage. In the same way, they assembled and checked themselves from stories and poems, from their memories, from one another's talk. . . . The search for indestructible landmarks in a destructible world led many down strange paths. The attachment to these when they had been found produced small worlds-within-worlds of hallucination—in most cases, saving hallucination.

This description of how people responded to the destruction of war is based on Miss Bowen's own experience, for at this time she found in Bowen's Court the "necessary illusion—peace at its most ecstatic" to "sustain" her through the war. The war "made [her] this image out of a house built of anxious history." Her writing the history of her family home, as well as that of her early childhood at 15 Herbert Place, and of her reading *(English Novelists,* 1946) points out again the connection between private imaginative fantasy and art that she felt in her own life. This connection explains why she wrote some of her best short stories at this time. "A Love Story: 1939," "Summer Night," "Ivy

Gripped the Steps," and "The Happy Autumn Fields" beautifully support Miss Bowen's claim that "Man has to live how he can: overlooked and dwarfed he makes himself his own theatre," and that the short story is freer than the novel "to measure man by his own aspirations and dreads and place him alone on that stage which, inwardly, every man is conscious of occupying alone."

Elizabeth Bowen described the stories in *The Demon Lover* as "flying particles of something enormous and inchoate"; she wanted her novel *The Heat of the Day,* which she was writing at the same time, "to be comprehensive." But "for the form's sake," she had to make "relentless exclusions," and the subsequent form of this novel is simple, even melodramatic. Rather than through structural design, it approaches the comprehensive only at certain finely achieved dramatic moments when one feels through the wartime particular "the high voltage current of the general pass."

The novel "spot-lights" those who were in London during the war, but who were, as Miss Bowen put it, not "the great sufferers" of its destruction. Stella Rodney is an attractive upper-middle-class divorceé in her forties, whose former husband is deceased, and whose twenty-year-old son, Roderick, is in training in the Army. She has been in love with Robert Kelway for two years, since the terrible bombings of September 1940, and she is pursued by a strange and disturbing man, also named Robert, but called Harrison throughout their relations, who tells her that Robert Kelway is passing secrets to the enemy and that Harrison will turn him in unless Stella agrees to give up Kelway and take Harrison as her lover. As Kelway and Harrison are matched in their ultimately destructive relations to Stella, so, too, is Stella doubled in the "cut-out" gestures of Louie Lewis, Miss Bowen's only portrait of a lower-class working girl. Louie's husband is away fighting in the war, leaving her, after the deaths of her parents, to her factory job alone in London. This balanced grouping of the characters serves to emphasize the discoveries of some that the others are not what they seemed. Stella's forced acceptance of Robert's treachery is matched by the discovery that after all Harrison did not want her but only the pleasure of calculating for her, and by Roderick's discovery that neither of his parents is what he had been raised to believe, and finally by Louie's disillusioned judgment that Stella was not a "virtuous" woman.

Because disruption, dislocation, and destruction are the actual condition of all life in *The Heat of the Day,* the legitimate terrors of darkened, bombed-out London during the war justify the characters' intensified feelings of insecurity, and the machinations of spy, counterspy intrigue exaggerate their feelings of conspiracy, plot, and betrayal. In this novel Elizabeth Bowen's language of violence, destruction, and conspiracy is literal; it is no longer metaphoric. The outward order of time and space is destroyed and life goes on in a vacuum; the war is a sea of horor through which the characters move, like fish in "shoals," among shored-up ruins.

In such a world, Roderick, Stella's son, is unusually fortunate in being provided with "what might be called an historic future" in the inheritance of Mount Morris, an Irish country house. The house and Ireland become for Roderick, another only child, what Bowen's Court was to Miss Bowen, something to cling to. Roderick has never seen this house, and by standing geographically outside of the war, it seems also to stand outside of the present, and thus of time, eternal. "The house, inhuman, became the hub of his imaginary life, of fancies, fantasies only so to be called because circumstances outlawed them from reality." The stability of this image, precisely because it is an image free from the tensions, deceptions, and mortality of human life, makes Roderick's fantasy of Mount Morris "saving," for it enables him to go on through the war. As Miss Bowen is always saying, but especially about life during the war, "after all, we had to go on *some* way."

What the house comes to be for Roderick, Robert is to Stella—"a habitat." "The lovers had for two years possessed a hermetic world, which, like the ideal book about nothing, stayed itself by its inner force." Because, as Miss Bowen has remarked before, every love has "a poetic relevance of its own," the rubble of wartime London becomes to Robert and Stella only part of "the junk-yard of what does not matter," and that " 'time being' which war had made the very being of time" allows their romantic love to remain afloat, like a bubble, on "this tideless, hypnotic, futureless day-to-day." So their world of love also seems hermetically sealed off from the war, out of time and space, and under the circumstances of the war that seems to suffice. But it is threatened, as Stella fearfully recognizes when, early in their love, she awakes one morning suddenly terrified that something may have happened to Robert during the night's bombing. The shock she experiences is the familiar "breaking down of immunity"; unlike Mount Morris, safely in Ireland out of London and the war, Robert, the hub of Stella's imaginary life, is not safe, and the narrative of their love is not free from reality.

Here Elizabeth Bowen again dramatizes the fundamental paradox of illusions of peace and security in love: because they include another human life, they actually increase one's vulnerability at the same time that they create a sense of immunity. The threats to Robert's life serve to increase the power of love to create an illusion of a private, safe world inhabited by only the two of them, just as the sense of immunity from war's dangers increases the feelings of susceptibility. This complementary effect is, however, produced by the belief that the deadly threat is external; external danger may be finally irreparable if and when it comes, but in the meantime it can be dealt with simply by thinking of something else. The appearance of Harrison shows that the threat to Stella and Robert's love comes not from the external danger of bombs, but from the war's existence inside the habitat of love, like the snake in the garden; the war's deceit, chaos, and inhumanity are revealed in the love itself. In this way Stella learns that " to have turned away from everything to one face is to find oneself face to face with everything." They have never been alone in their love because " they were the creatures of history, whose coming together was of a nature possible in no other day—the day was inherent in the nature."

Harrison is a man without feeling, incapable of receiving it or respecting it; as he says to Stella, *"I*

calculate—that's my life." The war has created a time
when he is not "a crook," for life now fully belongs to
those who calculate. When he comes to Stella with his
report on Robert and his proposition for her to save
him, Stella at first just refuses to believe him. She
exhibits that "sort of hardiness" she wears as "a poor
resource" along with all of her generation—Miss
Bowen's—which "as a generation had come to be made
to feel it had muffed the catch." Despite Stella's
determination to believe that "Such things do not
happen," and not to believe Harrison or even to believe
in him, what Harrison does is to involve her in his
suspicious view of life and in the internal reality
of espionage. He "distorts" love for her and makes
her a spy on Robert, seeking to check Harrison's
story. Later she tells him "You may not feel what
it feels like to be a spy; I do—ever since you came
to me with that story." What had been external and
threatening, "the grind and scream of battles,
mechanized advances excoriating flesh and country,"
has become internalized; the "war of dry cerebration"
inside the "windowless walls" of their consciousnesses is
where the true danger lies. "No act was not part of some
calculation; spontaneity was in tatters; from the point
of view of nothing more than the heart any action was
enemy action now." Our imaginary refuges and defenses
against external chaos and physical danger are not built
solely against those threats in themselves; they are built
also to prevent the battened down forces inside ourselves from being released and taking us over, making a
war within.

When Harrison convinces Stella of the truth of his

charges against Robert, she says to Louie, whom she meets by chance in a drearily inhuman downstairs cafe, so brilliantly lit as to be without shadows, "At any time...you or I may be learning some terrible human lesson which is to undo everything we had thought we had. It's that, not death, that we ought to live prepared for." Harrison is described as existing outside the fictional conventions for ordinary life; he must be the one to teach this woman, with all her hardiness, this terrible human lesson, which is terrible precisely because it seems, like Harrison himself, inhuman, "without any possible place in the human scene."

Robert Kelway, the traitor revealed by Harrison's calculating pursuit, is, in his own way, like Harrison, outside the human scene as Stella conceives of it. The discovery of his secret life undoes everything she thought she had, not simply because by being secret it was a betrayal of her and their love, but because it was a betrayal of her country and her ideals as well. When Robert finally admits his guilt to Stella, he tells her that "there are no more countries left" and that therefore there is no such thing as betrayal; "Don't you understand that all that language is dead currency?" Robert has "immunized" himself against this language of public feeling, just as Harrison has immunized himself against private feeling and expressions of it. To Robert, freedom is a "racket," in which suckers are "kidded along from the cradle to the grave," becoming "the muddled, mediocre, damned." He is willing to betray England to Germany, but he sees the Nazis only as destroyers necessary to the creation of a strong new order that will fulfill his great hunger to be. "We must have something to envisage, and we must act, and there must be law. We must have law—if necessary let it break us: to have been broken is to have been something."

Wounded at Dunkirk, Robert sees himself as having been born wounded and raised in "a man-eating house" under the emasculating dominance of the feminine will of his mother and sister Ernestine. The vague ideal of strength and order that is the "something" he envisages is his own illusion, a counteraction to his whole life, and like all illusions it creates a new order for Robert to live in. He feels that it "undid fear" and "bred" his impotent father out of him, giving him "a new heredity." The danger of spying creates the illusion of security and strength for him because he does it so intensely in the belief that it is not a way out but "the way on"—"outside it there came to be nothing else." So Robert, too, finds "some way" in which to go on, and in her presentation of his whole family Miss Bowen illustrates a point she expressed directly in *Bowen's Court:* "subjection to fantasy and infatuation with the idea of power" are "toxic" and they manifest themselves similarly in private, family, and public life ("the private cruelty and the world war both have their start in the heated brain"). Mrs. Kelway and Ernestine's power of fantasy and fantasy of power and Robert's support of the Nazis as an assertion of his and his father's strength of manhood are both manifestations, along with Hitler's Germany, of the heated brain, the outsized will. "The outsize will is not necessarily an evil: it is a phenomenon. It must have its outsize outlet, its big task. If the right scope is not offered it, it must seize the wrong. . . ."

With her history of the Bowens in Ireland, this is Miss Bowen's most "comprehensive" work; it is her most ambitious attempt to connect her personal and imaginative concern with private worlds of illusion to the larger public life of national politics and international ideals. In her examination of the thin membranes uniting and separating the degrees of private and public neurosis, Elizabeth Bowen includes in *The Heat of the Day* a character considered, officially at least, to be insane. Cousin Nettie, wife of the man who willed Mount Morris to Roderick, is kept in a "home," and when Roderick goes to see her he notes that in its being what the manageress calls "a little world of our own," upon which the outside world is not to intrude, it is "no more peculiar than any other abode." He also discovers that there is nothing peculiar about Nettie's malady either; she is merely trying to keep herself from seeing that life is a sea of horror, as in the picture of the Titanic, 1912 , that she left behind in her drawing room. Neither Cousin Nettie's vision nor her method of going on are peculiar; they only exaggerate by degree the visions and strategies of all the other characters and produce a greater degree of success in removing her from life.

Elizabeth Bowen shows most clearly in this novel that every way of going on has its cost. This is certainly true of Cousin Nettie's sanctuary, which is also a form of incarceration, but all those who survive in this novel do so at some cost. When Roderick learns from Nettie that his father left Stella, rather than the other way round, he must accept the new knowledge that this *"was"* his father, and he must readjust his diminished ideas of his mother and himself according to this knowledge. Stella, when faced with this knowledge in Roderick, must reconsider her entire definition of herself based, since that time, on her preference to "sound like a monster than look like a fool." After Robert's death by either falling or jumping from Stella's roof while trying to escape Harrison, Stella's "poor resource" of "hardiness" seems finally poorer than ever, for it now has become an ultimate lack of feeling, of caring. When she is found again by Harrison, who mysteriously disappears at Robert's death only to reappear just as mysteriously later on, she is in a new apartment under new bombing attacks waiting to be married or killed; it does not seem to matter which. She even offers to sleep with Harrison just to complete the bargain she had been willing to make with him to save Robert, but she discovers that Harrison does not really care about that, then or now. To go on now means just to forget, "one has got to forget—that is, if it is to be possible to live. The more wars there are, I suppose, the more we shall learn how to be survivors."

Art fails the characters in this novel; only nature goes on. Only Louie Lewis, disappointed to read in the newspaper account of Robert's death that Stella was not the "respectable" woman she needed to believe in, having to overcome the death of her husband in battle following on the deaths of her parents by bombs, pregnant by a unknown lover, seems to go on instinctively. Inarticulate, her "hardiness failed her," but this is what saves her and makes it possible for her to endure. In the conception and birth of her child, in its "intention to survive," she feels but cannot express what is the only consolation in this novel of the *"desiccation* by war, of our day-to-day lives." "Life, it was to be seen, selected its own methods of going on."

III

After the war, in 1952, Elizabeth Bowen and Alan Cameron returned to Ireland to live at Bowen's Court; this long cherished dream was, however, shattered by Mr. Cameron's death in August of that year. Miss Bowen's actual return to the source of the peaceful image that sustained her during the war recalled the "anxious history" out of which it came; the house that provided her with "an historic future" came to burden her with a sense of the past and the impossible financial responsibility of maintenance. In the peace after the war, she was reminded again in a different way of "the passionate attachment of men and women to every object or image or place or love or fragment of memory with which his or her destiny seemed to be assured," for the big house is all of these at once. Its existence proved Miss Bowen's point that "nothing in Ireland is ever over," and that "in. . .Ireland, if you do not know the past you only know the half of any one's mind." Miss Bowen's next novel, *A World of Love* (1955), evokes what she felt as the "spell" of big house country life in Ireland, where "The indefinite ghosts of the past, of the dead who have lived here and pursued this same routine of life in these walls add something, a sort of order, a reason for living, to every minute and hour." It is to the power of this spell, to what Miss Bowen had earlier called "fantasy" or "hallucination," that she pays her homage in this novel, supporting her claim that "at no time, even in the novel, do I consider realism to be my forte."

A World of Love is generally considered the least successful and least popular of all Miss Bowen's works; it is a difficult novel because Miss Bowen was deliberately striving for a more elaborate "poetic" style to create the effects of "mirage-like shimmer" that she found in Ireland's light-consumed distances, and of fantasy that would permit spiritual presences to move in and out of life. The problem with the novel, despite the narrator's clear judgments at certain moments, is the fundamental ambiguity about what is going on. The novel makes the best critical sense when viewed as another exploration of the characters' fantasies, their "queered" relations to the past. But just as there are some real ghosts in *The Demon Lover* stories, so, too, are there moments in *A World of Love* when it seems that Miss Bowen ought to be, because she seems to desire to be, writing a straight mystery story about unambiguous spiritual presences, real mediums, and true possession. One feels that this language is not just a convenient vocabulary for Miss Bowen, not just available metaphor, but a genuine possibility. The difficulty of excessive style in the novel seems to be caused by Miss Bowen's not making up her mind about which way the story should go and trying, therefore, to have it both ways. Uncertainty permeates this novel and epitomizes the inescapable ambivalence of her Anglo-Irish sensibility.

A World of Love and *The Last September* are the only novels to be set entirely in Ireland and to focus on isolated big house life. In *The House in Paris* and *The Heat of the Day,* Ireland exists as a world apart from the central focus of the characters' lives; it is a world of escape, apparently out of time, eternal, and out of the spaces of Paris and London, more an image or ideal than an actual place. As its title suggests, *A World of Love* makes this quality of unreality the entire "world" of the novel. Miss Bowen remarks in *Bowen's Court* that every Irish country house that has remained in the same family, "with its stables and farm and gardens deep in trees at the end of long avenues, is an island—and, like an island, a world." Montefort, the small country house in the novel, is further a world of illusion created by love, for as Miss Bowen has demonstrated in her earlier works, the world of love is always a world of illusion. In *A World of Love* the "habitats" of house and love are combined to form a more intense and comprehensive fantasy. The house seems "half-asleep" in the dawn light that effects "a new world—painted, expectant, empty, intense."

Montefort is a world of love in the relations of the characters living in the house to its former owner, Guy, who was killed in World War I. Montefort is now owned by Guy's cousin, Antonia, who loved him and who inherited his house; the house is lived in by her illegitimate cousin Fred Danby, who knew and admired both Guy and Antonia as they were all growing up, and Lilia, Guy's British fiancée, whom Antonia has married to Fred. The relation between Antonia and the Danbys is "uncertain, never secure, never defined" and strangely lasting (it has gone on for twenty-one years), "owing perhaps to all parties' reluctance to sitting down and having anything out, or to binding themselves to anything hard-and-fast, or to thinking out anything better." Jane Danby is a typical Bowen heroine, although the child of the early and brief passion of this arranged marriage and her father's favorite, she spends her winters with Antonia, a photographer, in London. At age twenty, she has completed her education and has returned to Montefort with Antonia for their annual summer visit; Jane has "a face perfectly ready to be a woman's but not yet so." Jane's readiness causes her to look to her future, which is just as uncertain as the past of the adults who surround her, and, like the adults, she has acquired that Anglo-Irish "necessary unconcern. She had grown up amid extreme situations and frantic statements; and, out of her feeling for equilibrium, contrived to ignore them as far as possible." Especially at Montefort, this "feeling for equilibrium" takes the form of "an instinctive aversion from the past."

To Elizabeth Bowen Jane's reaction is understandable; it is part of the nature of life, of going on.

> Life works to dispossess the dead, to dislodge and oust them. . . . Their continuous dying while we live, their repeated deaths as each of us dies who knew them are not in nature to be withstood. . . . Greatest of our denials to them is a part to play: it appears that they now cannot touch or alter whatever may be the existent scene—not only are they not here to participate, but there would be disorder if they *were* here. Their being left behind in their own time caused estrangement between them and us, who must live in ours.

Life *must* work to dispossess the dead because they have a power to take over life and make it share the dead's isolation. This power of the past is built into life, as it is built into and preserved in the structure of Montefort. So Jane finds a packet of Guy's love letters to an unknown woman, neither Antonia nor Lilia, and to the narrator the letters "found her rather than she them." Jane's untested readiness to be a woman and enter her future encourages her to fall in love with Guy and to sense his presence among them. The sensation of his presence is also experienced by Antonia and Lilia, and it affects each of them separately and in their relations to one another as well as to Guy.

Ironically Jane's readiness for a future leads her to the past, or, if one accepts the view that the letters find her and that she becomes "possessed" by Guy, the past overtakes and becomes part of the present and the anticipated future. In this way Jane's situation shows how the eternal works against temporal things, an effect that Miss Bowen attributed to Ireland itself and to the power of all illusion and art. Guy's letters were written from Montefort and describe the place as it was then and is now; Jane thus sees it for the first time as a permanent world of art into which she moves out of her time. She exclaims aloud to Guy "Oh, here I *am!*" Jane experiences what is called "a vision" that is "poetically immortal," and this heightened sense of life and herself in it is what she desires, so it becomes for her more "real" than the life immediately around her. When she is invited to a dinner party by Lady Latterly, the nouveau riche owner of a neighboring castle, she views everything and everyone as "theatre," except for Guy, who appears to her, after she gulps down her first martinis, and seems the only other person alive among "these poor ghosts."

Jane is forced to see the nature of her fantasy by the intrusions of her avenging younger sister Maud, who parodies Jane's experience in her relation with an invisible friend Gay David. Maud asks Jane when she comes upon her sequestered with her packet of letters down by the river, "What are *you* playing?" She is also mocked by the rather bitter Antonia, who makes sour remarks about Jane's "falling in love with a love letter." Maud's stealing of the letters finally shows Jane how unable she is to sustain her vision alone against the forces of the actual world around her. Fantasies, if they can be saving, can also be distracting and ultimately destructive. "Obstinate rememberers of the dead seem to queer themselves or show some sign of a malady. . . ." If life does not work to dispossess the dead, it becomes possessed and deadened by it.

The obstinate rememberers of Guy are Antonia and Lilia, who are all the more "queered" because their remembrance is suppressed. The uncertainty of their arrangements is continued in the unconscious expectation that Guy might perhaps return. Antonia, especially, cannot accept the incompleteness of Guy's untimely death, and her commitment to Montefort, the Danbys, and Jane is the expression of her own sense of incompleteness and her attempt to compensate for it. She has attempted to satisfy the "annihilating need left behind by Guy" in her imperious control over all the other lives that his touched. This power is derived from and appropriate to Guy, who along with Antonia seemed to Fred capable of running the world. Antonia's moment of vision similar to Jane's heightens her sense of her own power, for she feels that she and Guy are together again and can run the world. Her possession by him enables her to possess the world with him as its "lordly owners." "What was returned to her was the sense of 'always'—the conviction of going on, on and on." Antonia's sense of herself as a continuous identity, almost a cosmic force, is dependent on Guy. Her sense of him is what enables her to make herself felt by others, just as she now feels that she might make Fred her lover as she had previously made him Lilia's husband.

Lilia's acceptance of the uncertainty of the Danbys' arrangement with Antonia is more desperate than Antonia's because her memory of Guy is more uncertain. For her "not memories was it but expectations which haunted Montefort. [Guy's] immortality was in their longings. . .." Although Lilia knows that Guy and Antonia loved, she can think of herself as having replaced Antonia in his affections. But she cannot overcome the sense of loss of Guy because she knows that he was looking for someone other than Antonia or herself at the station after his last leave; Jane's uncovering of the letters to an unknown woman and becoming "Guy's latest love," and Antonia's recovered power all threaten her. Her sense of herself and all her subsequent relations to Antonia and Fred and Montefort depend on her role as the Beloved: "if not the Beloved, what was Lilia? Nothing. Nothing was left to be." One hot, glaring static day in Clonmore, Lilia is overcome by the hellish sensation that she literally cannot be. Elizabeth Bowen is clearest about the nature of Lilia's vision of Guy and its relation to reality. When alone in the garden, Lilia senses Guy's presence, just as Jane and Antonia have, but as she goes to meet it, she discovers Fred, her husband. Fred takes her out of the garden to give her the packet of letters that Maud had stolen from Jane and he, in turn, has taken from her. Fred's appearance with the letters at this moment allows Lilia to face up to Guy's infidelity, thereby ousting Guy, and at the same time to transfer all of her anticipations in the garden to Fred. Her love can now be given entirely to Fred, and this possibility of a new life and new identity for Lilia is represented by their first honest discussion of Lilia's past. This is Lilia's only possibility to be. "Survival seemed more possible now, for having spoken to one another had been an act of love."

Lilia's survival is thus a creative act; it is not deadening forgetfulness, as is Stella's survival at the end of *The Heat of the Day*. Lilia's act of life against death sets the pattern for similar experiences of life dispossessing the dead in Jane and Antonia. It affects Jane most directly, for she sees her mother and father together at this moment framed in the carriage archway, her mother holding Jane's lost packet of letters. At this moment Jane feels the characteristic Bowen sense of loss: "the worst of loss is when it at the same time is an enlightenment—that is what is not to be recovered from; ignorance cannot be made good." Jane's parents are now together as man and woman in love, not just as Jane's parents who love her. In seeing the letters Jane loses the Guy of her vision; he, too, "had finished his course here." Jane is "doomed," like all human beings, to knowledge, but the ambiguity of whether Jane found

Guy or Guy Jane is, however, continued by the narrator, "which of them dead man and living girl had been the player, and which the played with?"

These acts of discovery give to both Lilia and Jane what the narrator calls, "a new air of making [their] own terms." Such an autonomous sense of self naturally limits Antonia's sense of limitless power over them, and the moment of change for them all is signaled by Maud's radio transmitting the sound of Big Ben from London, bringing into Montefort the world of space and time. Antonia knows that what the clock meant was "Enough!" She accepts what has been, understanding that "one is never quite quit of what one has done," and she can now look toward the future on its own terms: "But for the future...we'd have nothing left." The final act for them all is Jane's burning of Guy's letters, the exorcising gesture of life dispossessing the dead as all the characters move out of eternal fantasy into time accepting that "nothing is so simple as you hope."

The novel's conclusion, which shows Jane going as a favor to meet a cast-off lover of Lady Latterly's, is a test of the reader's knowledge that nothing is so simple as one hopes or it appears. The final sentence of the book, "They no sooner looked but they loved," rather than providing a sentimental romantic ending to Jane's story, actually attests to the way illusions are perpetuated because they are necessary to life, and to the way one's "lookings–forward" may really be memories. There must not be a death of the heart. Jane's disillusioning experience of her too-ready love of the dead Guy cannot destroy her capacity for faith in the living imagination or love; it should only caution her to beware of distracting and destructive fantasy. So she, and the reader, must accept her actual circumstances and meet her possible fate with hope and faith and love, but also with wise skepticism.

Seven years after her return to Bowen's Court and the death of Alan Cameron, Elizabeth Bowen was forced by rising costs and her "anxiety, the more deep for being repressed," to sell the house that had sustained her through the war and the other crises of her life. She returned to Old Headington, Oxford, where she had lived for ten years shortly after her marriage, and there she wrote *The Little Girls.* After having returned to live permanently in Ireland, Miss Bowen returned to live permanently in England; having lost Bowen's Court and that part of her past, she returned to her past in Oxford. The book she wrote there is about women who return to their former relationships and their former school after fifty years of separation. Elizabeth Bowen calls these women "revenants," a word aptly descriptive of her own experience. *The Little Girls* is about what is lost in regaining the past and what is gained in losing it again; it was published in 1964, the same year as the revised edition of *Bowen's Court,* which concludes with an account of the house's demolition by the new owner.

The idea for *The Little Girls* may have come to Miss Bowen in writing *A World of Love,* for the relations of Jane, Antonia, and Lilia to Guy, to the past, and to one another are similar to the relations among the three women of *The Little Girls.* But there is nothing uncertain or overly elaborate about this book; it is Elizabeth Bowen's wittiest and funniest novel, and it retains the sense of mystery she sought in *A World of Love.* In this novel the return to the past is forced by Dinah Delacroix when she seeks out the two school girl friends who were closest to her during their last term at St. Agatha's in the summer of 1914. So in this novel someone in the present seeks out the past, rather than, as in *A World of Love,* someone from the past seeking out the present. *The Little Girls* is divided, like *The House in Paris,* into three parts, the first and last of which are in the present; the middle section describes the activities of fifty years ago, when the women were eleven-year-old girls at the end of their last school term. This apparently more natural movement from the present to the past, both in the lives of the characters and in the structure of the novel, does not however exclude the quality of mystery. On the contrary, the power that each of the three girls possesses over the other two, and especially Dinah's power in recalling the others, is seen as a form of witchcraft. The women in *The Little Girls* are seen by one another and their author as the witches in *Macbeth;* they come together not to announce Macbeth's fate, but because they are one another's fate. Chance not choice brings them together. This is the discovery of the novel both for the characters and the reader, but it is a discovery that reveals a fundamental, impenetrable mystery about human life.

Like Emmeline in *To The North,* Dinah does not seem desperate and yet she reaches the point of breakdown, which in this novel is saving rather than fatal. In the envious eyes of her friends Dinah seems to have everything; she has been successfully married, born two sons, who are now married themselves, and at sixty-one is still attractive. Her widowhood is enlivened by the admiration of a handsome, if somewhat sour and selfish widower, Frank, who is "nuts about her." She seems the sort of person who "gets everything she goes out for," and she exerts influence over the lives of people around her, even to the point of making them give up "expressive objects," things they have "obsessions about, keep on wearing or using, or fuss when they lose, or can't go to sleep without." She is first seen storing these objects in a cave that she plans to seal up for posterity in the hope of guaranteeing her and her friends' survival into the future as distinct personalities, rather than merely as a race or anthropological theory. This project and the sight of an off-balance swing make Dinah recall another childish attempt to preserve identity and baffle posterity that she shared at St. Agatha's with her friends Clare, then called "Mumbo," and Sheila, "Sheikie." As "Dicey" she impulsively advertises for them in *The Times* and local newspapers, sensing that the cave and the swing in her present life were only "precipitants." "WE were the start of this," she tells them when they meet, and concludes "We are posterity, now."

The project of the little girls at St. Agatha's was to bury a coffer containing a cryptic message written in blood in a code worked out by Mumbo (Mumbo-Jumbo) and various symbolic objects, including, at Sheikie's demand, a possession of each girl known only to herself. Dinah's present plan is to recall the other girls and to return and dig up the coffer. Clare and Sheila try to resist Dinah's efforts to find them, but they are forced by increasingly embarrassing advertisements to agree to meet her. Clare, who is divorced, owns and manages a small but successful chain of Mopsie Pie gift shops; Sheila is barrenly married to the younger son of her father's real estate partner, and she lives in Southstone (Folkstone), the site of St. Agatha's, decorously restrained by family pride and social position. The women resist Dinah's pressure because they believe they have outgrown their childhood and because they are suspicious of their ability to retain their adult identities against the power of their old friendship. But the force of Dinah's initiative is too strong, and their present adult lives are made to disappear as the three, reunited, resume their old intimacy and nicknames and come to live under their shared spell. As soon as they meet they are "back where they had left off"; even heterosexual love no longer counts: "Those were the days before love. These are the days after. Nothing has gone for nothing but the days between," says Clare.

Such is the power of their bond; again the power of illusion, of love, and of art continues to fascinate Elizabeth Bowen's imagination, but the language of aesthetic creation now merges with that of witchcraft and magic. What remains constant is Miss Bowen's consciousness of her own metaphor-making and her frequent desire—in *The Little Girls* her brilliant source of comic irony—to make the reader share in her own spell-casting by undercutting it with commonplace utterances and occurrences. If on one level we are invited to see these women and their shared power as the witches from *Macbeth,* we are also forced at the same time but on another level to see them as just naughty little girls. As Dinah's mother says about the girls' attempt to blow up Sheikie's bicycle shed, "It couldn't possibly be—could it—that you're bad for each other?"

Although Clare and Sheila consider Dinah's plan to return to dig up their treasure as absurd and are determined not to attempt it, Dinah succeeds in persuading them. St. Agatha's has been gone since the war, and, so, too, the women discover by flashlight, are the contents of the treasure box. The effect of the empty coffer on the imperious Dinah is surprising and puzzling to the other women. "Can't you see what's happened? This us three. This going back, I mean. This began as a game, *began* as a game. Now—you see?—it's got me!" More startling and frightening is Dinah's collapse after the tough Clare refuses to accompany her home to live with her. When Dinah is found by her houseboy and Frank, she is crying, "It's all gone, was it ever there? No, never there. Nothing. No, no, no. . . ." It is only later that Clare comes to understand that the return to the box and its emptiness with no notion of what happened to the contents constituted an identity crisis for Dinah: "There being nothing was what you were frightened of all the time, eh? Yes. Yes, it was terrible looking down into that empty box." The sense of emptiness at the core of herself and her life back somewhere in her past is what Dinah unconsciously felt and needed to test, hopefully, to be reassured. But the void was mysteriously confirmed rather than dispelled or filled. This discovery reverses the reader's view of Dinah shared with Clare and Sheila.

The return to the past reveals to Dinah that it has

disappeared, and this loss makes her adult life, which seemed so full, so "nice and fun" as Sheila puts it, seem unreal. Her maturity is shown to be the illusion, the magic trick, the sham, the game—terms which recur in the novel. Clare tells Dinah that she is "a cheat. A player-about. Never once have you played fair, all along the line. . . ." But Dinah is the one to suffer most by her cheating game. Her essential self is bound up with that life at St. Agatha's years ago. The mystery of that life, but not the disappearance of the coffer's contents, is illuminated in retrospect by Clare's calling Dinah a "Circe" and an "enchantress's child." These allusions refer to the relation between Clare's father and Dinah's mother, which corresponds chronologically to the relation of the little girls just before the war and prophesies, if not determines, the relation between Clare and Dinah suggested at the conclusion of the novel.

When the girls were at St. Agatha's, Dinah and her mother, Mrs. Piggot (the Circe allusion again), lived in a small cottage surrounded by fine, repaired china and books. This world of "things" attracts the rootless Army child Clare, but the attraction is not simply that of a tangible sense of security; it is ambivalently also the suggestion of loss, and of vague spooky threat. Mrs. Piggot and Dinah had "spun round themselves a tangible web, through whose transparency, layers deep, one glimpsed some fixed, perhaps haunted, other dimension." Later, Dinah reveals that her father killed himself by throwing himself under a train, and when Dinah collapses and thinks of Macbeth, she will say to Sheila " 'Was my father a traitor, mother?'—that's Macbeth." This pointed reference identifies the "fixed, haunted, other dimension" deep in the lives of both Mrs. Piggot and her child. The sense of betrayal, so fundamental in all Miss Bowen's fiction, is what works in Dinah as a child and as an adult, both as a power to attract and influence others and as a fear that ultimately undermines her sense of self and reality.

Clare's father is also attracted to this "web" created by Mrs. Piggot, and, before going off to the war in which he will be killed, he tells her surreptitiously at the girls' last picnic on the beach that she is "cold." She attracts Major Burkin-Jones, but she cannot satisfy his love. The shock of her first husband's suicide and perhaps her sense of responsibility for it keep her from loving. When Clare asks Dinah why her mother did not remarry, she replies "There are shocks you do not take the risk of twice." This numbing coldness in Mrs. Piggot is designed to be protective, and for this reason it appeals to Clare, who does not wish to be "overcome" by any emotion, for "to be overcome is to be got the better of." Dinah loves Clare, but as a child Mumbo does not say good-bye to her that last day on the beach, and as an adult she will not accept Dinah's pleas that she come live with her. Clare's refusal, following upon the discovery of the empty coffer, is the immediate cause of Dinah's collapse. The two in a fixed haunted way seem to be caught not only in the spell of their childhood but in the relations between their parents during their childhood. The past is never over, and it is just the unconsummated, exasperating nature of the love between their parents that lives on in the relations between the women. Dinah asks "Does it ever seem to you that the non-sins of our fathers—and mothers— have been visited upon us?"

As a child Dinah attempted to exorcise the peril of love by placing a revolver in the coffer as her private item, or totem. She attempts literally to bury the violence of the love in her life, and so, at least until the beginning of the novel when she is sixty-one, she goes on to a life of love and happiness. The sense of peril and violence returns with the return to the past and the discovery that it is no longer buried. Clare's reaction is comparable, but it takes a different form; she buries a copy of Shelley in the coffer, for her strategy for coping is to eliminate the poetry, the passion, and therefore the risk from her life. She goes on to a life of successful business enterprise. But the passion and the poetry, even her Mumbo-Jumbo, return to her with Dinah and the past; in being lost from the box, they are found. At first she resists and again hurts—this time almost destroys—Dinah, who says "you huffed and you puffed and you blew my house down." But Clare can now see what she has done, and she says standing over the bed where Dinah sleeps after her collapse: "I did not comfort you. Never have I comforted you. Forgive me." Clare's recognition of what she has become and of her own responsibility for what has happened to Dinah is complemented by Dinah's awakening from her sleep and from her frightening trip into the past and her vision of the void to a proper sense of her life in the present as an adult. She asks "Who's there?" "Mumbo," "Not Mumbo. Clare. Clare, where have you been?"

This moment is both a moment of loss and recovery that contains the action of the entire novel. Dinah and Clare have regained their paradise, recaptured their past, by losing it. Dicey and Mumbo are gone; Dinah and Clare, who were and are those two little girls, remain, but they are something more now, too. They are adults ready to accept the risk of love. They both have regained Sheikie in a Sheila, who comes to care for Dinah during her collapse, and who finds in caring for Dinah a way of meeting her sense of guilt for having left the sickroom of her lover on the day of his death. In addition to Dinah and Clare, Sheila also finds the children and busyness and fun she never had in her marriage in the admiration of Dinah's sons. The amputated sixth toe, which she put in the coffer and never told anyone about, indicated her former inability to accept her fate. She now seems cheerfully willing to do so—as they all must as adults, for they are one another's fate.

> We were entrusted to one another in the day which mattered, Clare thought. Entrusted to one another by chance, not choice. Chance, and its agents time and place. Chance is better than choice, it is more lordly. In its carelessness it is more lordly. Chance is God, choice is man. You—she thought looking at the bed—chanced, not chose, to want us again.

The naughty little girls, the funny tragic witches, discern and accept the mystery of their fate as Elizabeth Bowen must have done when she had to give up Bowen's Court and then had to witness its demolition. This was the fate of her family house and of her long, loving, troublesome relation to it; this loss, too, was a gain. Miss Bowen gained a freedom from the anxiety about the house that had even prevented her from writing. But more significantly, this loss of the house allowed her to gain it back in a complete and perfect way—by making it exclusively into memory and art. In

The Little Girls, when the women return to the grounds of the vanished St. Agatha's, Miss Bowen says "There is seldom anything convulsive about change. What is there is there; there comes to be something fictitious about what is not." This is the sense one gets from the revised edition of *Bowen's Court;* the book had been written as history and memory and it had now become pure image, pure art. The house reached its apotheosis through its destruction."When I think of Bowen's Court, there it is. . . There is a sort of perpetuity about livingness. . . ." This knowledge is what replaces the missing objects in the coffer; it is what fills the void; it is how, Miss Bowen tells us, we live. As Dinah states it in *The Little Girls,* "It's by picturing things that one lives. . . ." This is art and magic; the art of magic and the magic of art.

Like the revenants in *The Little Girls,* Miss Bowen went even further back into her past when, in 1965, she returned to Hythe, Kent, where she had settled with her mother nearly sixty years before. Here she wrote her tenth and last novel, *Eva Trout* (1969), and it is a recapitulation of all Miss Bowen's personal and fictional experiences of anguished insecurity. It is the only novel whose title is that of the name of the main character, and Eva Trout is Miss Bowen's only full-scale treatment of a truly neurotic heroine. In Eva Trout, all of the isolated and isolating, the self-destructive and destructive capacities of all her innocent heroines are concentrated and exaggerated. She is that most distinct and proverbial alien, a fish out of water, desperately and recklessly flopping about for survival.

Eva Trout, like Miss Bowen's other heroines, is defined by the disordered circumstances of her parents' lives. She is first of all, an only child, and she is alone because she is an orphan. These are the primary conditions and metaphors for Miss Bowen's consideration of the crisis of identity which recurs throughout her work. Moreover, Eva is a lonely only child because she has been betrayed early in her life; her mother left her shortly after Eva's birth; she is "motherless from the cradle," but she claims to remember her mother's shriek. This shriek and her mother's desertion were caused by her discovery of Willy Trout's homosexual love affair with a repulsive—immobile, fleshy, blond, and pinkish—associate named Constantine. Eva's mother was killed in a plane crash after her desertion of her family, and Eva was later abandoned by her father, who committed suicide because of Constantine's cruelty to him. As Iseult, one of Eva's teachers and early loves puts it, "What an ambience to grow up in, a hated love. What isolation round them."

Eva's childhood is, then, more disordered and violent than one comes to expect even in the novels of Elizabeth Bowen. The effect of these violent separations and losses and the constant moving about and living in hotels with governesses is that the ordinary appearance of adult conspiracy that the child cannot comprehend is intensified to the point of actual disorientation. Eva's original condition of being an abandoned only child thus becomes merged with another of Miss Bowen's favorite metaphors, that of the "displaced person." Eva's identity is not divided or confused by two places, such as Ireland and England; it is diffused among so many as to create a sense of not being, as in not being "all there." Eva cannot even experience the ordinary childhood feeling of being homesick, "for, homesick for where?" As Eva pathetically says to Iseult, "anywhere would seem strange to me that did not seem strange."

Another condition of Eva's situation is a complement to the others and still another of Miss Bowen's metaphors for life. Just as Eva cannot make connections among the places she has been to give her a sense of meaningful continuity in her life, so, too, she cannot make connections among her thoughts and feelings or between herself and others through language. Miss Bowen's speech was afflicted by a stammer from the time of her childhood traumas, and Eva, "the monstrous heiress," is "unable to speak—talk, be understood, converse." She cannot join things together, "this, then that, then the other," and her choice of diction is startling and confusing. More than any of Miss Bowen's other innocents, Eva literally can find no language in which to speak on her own terms, and she does not resign herself to being translated imperfectly. Rather, she seeks what she imagines to be the perfection of "normal" patterns of behavior and speech in order to overcome her psychic fragmentation ("To reassemble the picture was impossible; too many of the pieces were lost, lacking").

When Iseult takes an interest in Eva at school, Eva is reluctant to respond, even though she is attracted by this "attention [that] could seem to be love." In accordance with the implied imagery of Eva's family name, Iseult asks her to come nearer the surface, though, "there are some times when I think you would rather go on submerged." In responding that she fears Iseult will "find out. . . I have nothing to declare," Eva implies that she will have nothing to say because she is no one, but also that she has nothing to declare at customs, that she brings with her nothing of value. (The fear of customs officials was one of Miss Bowen's concerns as an outsider, an alien, and becomes a metaphor for all complex people, "never certain their passports are in order.") So Eva either stays at her own depths, alone; or, surfacing at the "lure" of someone's affection or "dragged up" from her depths into the "airs" of corrupt affections which are systematized into manners and conventional expectations, she in her awkward, "monstrous" way "fancies" the expected patterns for her life.

She sets out to acquire the tangible signs of acceptable identity, a home complete with husband and child. But characteristically she mixes up the acceptable order, and she is satisfied with fictions instead of facts, with appearance instead of reality—as are, of course, the landlubbers around her. But they find her so disturbing and call her disturbed, insane, because her innocently ruthless pursuit of such fictions makes her dangerous, not only to others but also to herself: "You are artless; that is the awful thing. You roll round like some blind deflectible planet. *Sauve qui peut,* those who are in your course."

Those in Eva's course are Iseult and her husband Eric Arble, Henry Dauncey, a young neighbor of the Arbles, and Jeremy, her secretively and illegally acquired child. At the beginning of the novel, Eva, approaching her twenty-fifth birthday and her inheritance from her successful financier father, is staying as a paying guest with her former schoolmistress, Iseult, and her husband on their failed fruit farm. As the fruit farm failed, so is the fruitless marriage failing; it was founded on "a cerebral young woman's first physical passion," a cerebral young woman who "had been a D. H. Lawrence reader and was a townswoman." Although Iseult is genuinely concerned about Eva, Eva's presence in the Arbles' home reflects their need for money and their attempt to distract themselves from their own marital problems. But Eva naturally complicates rather than alleviates these problems. Moreover, she now feels in Iseult's less concentrated and more cautious attention the beginnings of another betrayal. Eva says later that "She abandoned me. She betrayed me. ... She betrayed my hopes, having led them on. She pretended love, to make me show myself to her—then, thinking she saw all, she turned away."

What Eva resents most of all is her lost sense of becoming ("I was *Beginning* to be") and her feeling of being lost again, of being no one nowhere. She feels Iseult "sent me back again— to be nothing. . . .I remain gone. Where am I? I do not know—I was cast out from where I believed I was." Eva, like her namesake Eve, in her desire to be, which is to know, and to love and be loved, has been cast out of her Eden, which is the fruit farm, by the satanic forces of deception and betrayal. Eva Trout is physically a large person; she is also figuratively large in her association with Eve; as one of the characters remarks to her, her persona is "outsize, larger-than-life in every way. That's how you fascinate the imagination." Miss Bowen's imagination has always been fascinated by the story of the fall because it is larger than life.

Eva responds to her expulsion by first seeking to recreate an Eden, locating herself for the first time in her life in a real place of her own. With her inheritance she buys a sturdy, sham-old house on the coast near Broadstairs; before she even sees it, she is calling it her "home," hoping that to be somewhere is to be someone. Conscious of having attracted some attention from the frustrated Eric, she allows herself to be found at her new home by him. He expresses his affection for her, but Eva replies that she cannot be his: " 'Never,' said Eva positively, 'have I been anyone's; so how could I be?' " Eva's refusal of this opportunity to be by being someone's is difficult to understand; it may be an honest response to Eric's confused expression of love; it may also be an instinctive aversion similar to that which took place when Iseult first paid attention to her at school, exaggerated by Iseult's betrayal. Eva, at any rate, now seems to place her hopes only in the inanimate furnished house, rather than in human relations. Later she seems more conscious of her need to communicate with others more satisfactorily than she does, and in her "rootless rich girl" way, she fills the drawing room with modern electronic communications equipment, stereo, movie projector, and tape recorder, none of which she ever uses.

Her next attempt at an acceptable fiction for being is to acquire a child, apparently on the assumption that children, with whom she has always gotten on better than with adults, are more likely to understand and appreciate her and less likely to betray her. Eric's visit does, however, provide her with a way of explaining her acquisition of a child and also of "getting back" at

Iseult for her betrayal. When Iseult comes to see Eva, to invite her to visit at Christmas, and to ask if the two could not "begin again," Eva allows her to assume that she is going to have a child by Eric.

Jeremy, the child that Eva acquires in America, is her symbolic double, and their relationship is an emblem of Eva's whole life as well as the literal end of it. Eva's isolation and inability to communicate are repeated in Jeremy's being a cast-off child sold on the black market and in his being a deaf mute. The child's physical disability, like Eva's psychic disabilities, has the effect of suggesting "an unearthly perspicacity" in him that makes others feel handicapped. Like Eva, he delights in making self-absorbing patterns of trashy things he finds, and their relation becomes one of "close, almost ceaseless companionship and constant, pensive mutual contemplation." In their reinforcement they are not so much mother and child as twins protected in a womb: "sublimated monotony had cocooned the two of them, making them near as twins in a womb." As they move from one American city to another, ostensibly looking for special medical help for Jeremy, which he persistently resists, and actually repeating Eva's childhood travels with her father before his suicide, they create and live in their own "cinemato-graphic existence, with no sound track." "The one wonder, to them, of the exterior world was that anything should be exterior to themselves— and *could anything be so and yet exist?"*

The answer, of course, is yes, and this discovery is the loss of this Eden, the "sundering" of the cocooned twins by their birth into the world exterior to their "story." After eight years, Eva decides to return to England with Jeremy. This return to her past life and her past acquaintances separates her from him, makes him an alien to their world and her to his. The boy feels this move as a betrayal, and he resents it just as Eva has resented her losses. "Eva had broken a pact, which was very grievous." The child's capacity for violence is shown in occasional tantrums, but its ultimate expression is foreshadowed in a warning from Constantine, who tells Eva that Jeremy hugs his disability because it is a form of immunity. "He does well with it—you make life too charming for him: an Eden. High time he was cast forth from it; as things are, that could only be done across your dead body."

The return to England is hardly comforting to Eva, for the familiarity of places and people only serves to emphasize the differences in their relations. The Arbles have separated, Eric is living with a Scandanavian woman by whom he has had two children, Iseult has gone to the continent, but returns because she is now in collusion with Constantine, whom she had previously distrusted. In the midst of her new confusion, Eva goes to visit the National Portrait Gallery; reconsidering the previously assumed "unreality" of the captured images there, she now thinks that every soul becomes only a portrait, that " there was no 'real life'; no life was more real than this." Only the "personae" remain the same; "there is no hope of keeping a check on people; you cannot know what they do, or why they do it. Situations alter for no knowable reason—as though a game continued while you were away from the table."

So Eva leaves England for Paris and later Fountainbleu, where Jeremy begins to respond to treatment for the first time. But Eva's "passion for the fictitious for its own sake" and the pressure of her friends to make her give "purpose" to her life now lead Eva to acquire a husband. Her choice is Henry Dauncey, another "kindred spirit" whom she had known since he was a child of twelve. Eva, Mrs. Dauncey says, is "a child at heart." She finds Henry at Cambridge, "a nebulous undergraduate of twenty," and in her imperious way she proposes marriage to him. Henry refuses, but Eva, grasping the need for the power of illusion, asks Henry only to pretend that he is going to marry her and to agree to depart from Victoria Station with her. Henry agrees, and Eva invites all of her acquaintances and lost Trout relatives to the ceremonial leave-taking. Even Jeremy, on holiday from France, is to be present for the occasion.

With the world all before her at Victoria, Eva Trout finally achieves her full being. Henry, who has cared about Eva all along—he's the only one who ever missed Eva—tells her that he does really wish to marry her; and for the first time in her life, the child who has suffered so much but never cried in grief, cries tears of joy. The girl who seemed "framed for happiness" is about to experience it as a woman in love. But to do so, is utterly to betray Jeremy, to end the universe they shared. Jeremy, with a pistol taken from Iseult, responds to the drama of this occasion by playfully acting out his part as betrayed. He fires the gun and kills Eva and ends the novel. They both leave their Eden over Eva's dead body; and once again the innocents become their own victims.

This violently melodramatic conclusion to the novel

has produced the harshest criticism of Miss Bowen's late fiction. But *Eva Trout* is a projection of psychic forces, which are by nature both violent and melodramatic. Miss Bowen's out-sized heroine, so rich and autonomous, so imperious even in her attempts to reduce herself to normal size, demands the elaborate sets of "changing scenes," the novel's subtitle, and theatrical moments such as the book's grand finale. The operatic names of the other characters and their controverted passions are the necessary complements to the desperate alienation of Eva. This is a Dickensian novel in its claustrophobia and also in its feelings of possession, of—what Constantine says of Eva—"dynamic energy seeking an outlet." This outlet is identity; it is what Eve and Eva had to be. What this novel, with its black humor, mischievous puns, and its own imperious willingness to ignore the conventional expectations for the realistic novel, conveys is that identity is energy. This is the final significance of Eva's last name; she is a fish out of water and that is precisely what makes her so difficult to handle. We cannot get hold of her until she is dead, until she is just an image. This is Elizabeth Bowen's final statement of her recurrent subject, "what a slippery fish is identity; and what *is* it besides a slippery fish?"

Selected Bibliography

WORKS BY ELIZABETH BOWEN

Encounters. [Short Stories] London: Sidgwick and Jackson, 1923; New York: Boni and Liveright, 1925. Republished with *Ann Lee's* in *Early Stories* (New York: Alfred A. Knopf, 1950).

Ann Lee's and Other Stories. London: Sidgwick and Jackson, 1926; New York: Boni and Liversight, 1926. Republished with *Encounters* in *Early Stories* (New York: Alfred A. Knopf, 1950).

The Hotel. London: Constable and Co., Ltd., 1927; New York: The Dial Press, Inc., 1928.

Joining Charles and Other Stories. London: Constable, 1929; New York: The Dial Press, 1929.

The Last September. London: Constable, 1929; New York: The Dial Press, 1929.

Friends and Relations. London: Constable, 1931; New York: The Dial Press, 1931.

To The North. London: Victor Gollancz, 1932; New York: Alfred A. Knopf, 1933.

The Cat Jumps and Other Stories. London: Victor Gollancz, 1934.

The House in Paris. London: Victor Gollancz, 1935; New York: Alfred A. Knopf, 1936.

The Death of the Heart. London: Victor Gollancz, 1935; New York: Alfred A. Knopf, 1936.

105

Look At All Those Roses. [Short Stories] London: Victor Gollancz, 1941; New York: Alfred A. Knopf, 1941.

Bowen's Court. [History] London: Longmans, Green & Co., 1942; New York: Alfred A. Knopf, 1942. Second edition, including Afterword: London: Longmans, Green & Co., 1964; New York: Alfred A. Knopf, 1964.

English Novelists. [Literary History] London: W. Collins, 1942.

Seven Winters: Memories of a Dublin Childhood. [Autobiography] Dublin: Cuala Press, 1942. Republished as *Seven Winters: Memories of a Dublin Childhood and Afterthoughts: Pieces on Writing* (New York: Alfred A. Knopf, 1962).

The Demon Lover and Other Stories. London: Jonathan Cape, 1945. Published in America with Preface as *Ivy Gripped the Steps* (New York: Alfred A. Knopf, 1946).

Anthony Trollope: A New Judgment. [Drama] New York and London: Oxford University Press, 1946.

Castle Anna. A Play, coauthored by John Perry. Unpublished. First performed in London, March, 1948.

Why Do I Write? An Exchange of Views Between Elizabeth Bowen, Graham Greene, and V.S. Pritchett. London: Percival Marshall, 1948.

The Heat of the Day. London: Jonathan Cape, 1949; New York: Alfred A. Knopf, 1949.

Collected Impressions. [Essays] London: Longmans, Green & Co.; New York: Alfred A. Knopf, 1950.

The Shelbourne: A Center in Dublin Life for More Than a Century. [History] London: George G. Harrap and Co., 1951. Published in America as *The Shelbourne Hotel* (New York: Alfred A. Knopf, 1951).

A World of Love. London: Jonathan Cape, 1955; New York: Alfred A. Knopf, 1955.

Stories by Elizabeth Bowen. New York: Alfred A. Knopf, 1959.

A Time in Rome. [Travel] New York: Alfred A. Knopf, 1960; London: Longmans, Green, & Co., 1960.

Afterthought: Pieces About Writing. London: Longmans, Green and Co., 1962. Published in America as *Seven Win-*

ters: Memories of a Dublin Childhood and After-thoughts: Pieces on Writing (New York: Alfred A. Knopf, 1962).

The Little Girls. London: Jonathan Cape, 1964; New York: Alfred A. Knopf, 1964.

A Day in the Dark and Other Stories. London: Jonathan Cape, 1965.

The Good Tiger. [Children's Book] New York: Alfred A. Knopf, 1965.

Eva Trout or Changing Scenes. New York: Alfred A. Knopf, 1968; London: Jonathan Cape, 1969.

SECONDARY STUDIES

Austin Alan E. *Elizabeth Bowen.* New York: Twayne Publishers, Inc., 1971.

Brooke, Jocelyn. *Elizabeth Bowen.* London: Longmans, Green & Co. for the British Council and the National Book League, 1952.

Hall, James. "The Giant Located: Elizabeth Bowen" in *The Lunatic Giant in the Drawing Room: The British and American Novel since 1930.* Bloomington: Indiana University Press, 1968.

Heath, William. *Elizabeth Bowen: An Introduction to Her Novels.* Madison: The University of Wisconsin Press, 1961.

Karl, Frederick. "The World of Elizabeth Bowen" in *The Contemporary English Novel.* New York: Farrar, Straus and Cudahy, 1962.

O'Faolain, Sean. "Elizabeth Bowen: Romance does not pay" in *The Vanishing Hero: Studies in Novelists of the Twenties.* London: Eyre and Spottiswood, 1956.

Sellery, J'Nan. "Elizabeth Bowen: A Check List," *Bulletin of the New York Public Library* 74 (April 1970): 219-74.

*NOTE: Only first English and American editions of Elizabeth Bowen's works are listed, except where later editions are of special interest. Most of Miss Bowen's work is published in the United States by Alfred A. Knopf, New York; in England Miss Bowen's fiction is published in a Collected Edition by Jonathan Cape, London.